Making Mosaics
WITH
Found
Objects

D1200963

0 11557 00615 5

Making
Mosaics
WITH
Found
Objects

...

MARA WALLACH

STACKPOLE
BOOKS

In memory of my father Eddie, who convinced me that "can't" isn't a word.

Copyright © 2010 by Stackpole Books

Published by
STACKPOLE BOOKS
5067 Ritter Road
Mechanicsburg, PA 17055
www.stackpolebooks.com

Printed in China

10 9 8 7 6 5 4 3 2 1

First edition

Cover design by Caroline Stover

Library of Congress Cataloging-in-Publication Data

Wallach, Mara.
    Making mosaics with found objects / Mara Wallach.
  — 1st ed.
      p.   cm.
    ISBN 978-0-8117-0615-5
    1. Glass craft. 2. Mosaics. 3. Salvage (Waste, etc.)
4. Found objects (Art) I. Title.
TT298.W354   2010
748.5—dc22

                        2010026230

Contents

The Tiled Path

"I found I could say things with color and shapes that I couldn't say any other way—things I had no words for." —Georgia O'Keeffe

The day that I threw caution to the wind and just started gluing stuff to other stuff, questions arose that I was unable to answer. Now, more than twenty years later, through trial and error, I have found my creative comfort zone, where I can create with reckless abandon. Nothing is safe from me and my glue.

There are many mosaic tile artists that I admire, and I've had the honor of taking classes from a few of them. Without exception, every class I've taken has taught me something that either saves me a great deal of time or provides just the creative permission I need to learn a new technique and nurture my creative self.

My attraction to china, tile, found objects, and castoffs has

Laurel Skye is one of the great mosaic tile artists I have taken classes with.

brought a lot of joy (and a little clutter) into my life. At times, it can become overwhelming. There is so much cool stuff to glue, so many ways to glue it, and so little time. A piece of chipped china can be reincarnated a thousand ways. But that's the beauty of the craft: old things become new again, and discarded objects hold renewed value.

This is a whimsical and random journey with infinite possibilities. Anyone, and I mean anyone, can create a masterpiece of found objects that will ignite the creative spirit. Whether it's a funky random declaration or a fine arts finished piece, it's all good!

This book was written as a basic guide to the world of mosaic tile and found objects. I've included many of the tips, tricks, and techniques that I've learned along the way. I hope this book will help to answer many of the questions that you may have regarding this art form, and blow a little breeze of creative inspiration your way, too.

The projects in this book were designed with beginners in mind. They involve just enough cutting to give you a gentle push, providing the momentum you need to begin your own journey down the tiled path.

Like any respectable pilgrimage or expedition, when you begin this journey you must take an oath. You have to acknowledge that you're creative, or at least promise never to say that you're not creative (even if you claim to have only bought this book for the pictures).

Everyone is blessed with creativity, even if you haven't discovered it yet. Mosaic tile and found object art is the best way to prove your nay-saying self wrong. Fear of artistic exposure can be intimidating. Just performing the process and putting it out there for all to see takes courage. But since there isn't one right way to do this, what have you got to lose?

The basic mosaic tile process I use

- Find the base.
- Choose a color palette and theme.
- Gather materials—tile, china, jewelry, buttons, game pieces, stained glass, other glass, marbles, gems, and stones—that fit into your chosen palette.

Mosaic Basics

- **Don't like what you've glued? Remove it.**
- **Grout color wrong? Live with it.**

- Prepare the surface properly, to get the pieces to stick securely— it's worth the extra effort!
- Start moving the pieces around until you reach a design that you're happy with.
- Cut materials to fit into the design you've decided on. If pieces don't lie flat, cut them smaller.
- When you're happy with your design, start gluing your project with the appropriate adhesive. If it's a larger project with many sides, glue the shards in sections, allowing drying time before moving on to the next area.

■ Let the glued surface dry a mini-
mum of 24 hours.
■ Grab your grout, water and/or
additive, and disposable gloves.
■ Grout.
■ Clean the grout from the piece.

You can paint grout with acrylic paints if you want—after it's dry, of course. Painting grout can be very messy and tedious, but it is doable.

- Let the grout dry.
- Polish with a soft lint-free cloth.
- Enjoy.
- Admire.
- Smile.

Pique Assiette

The term **pique assiette** was originally applied to the art of making mosaics with the pieces of broken plates. It is now often used for any kind of mosaic making.

Basic Techniques

Materials

You don't have to go very far to find cool materials and quirky found objects you can use in mosaics: old keys, jewelry, knick-knacks, medals, buttons, small toys, game pieces, old china, ceramic tile, and stained glass, just to name a few.

Tesserae *n. pl.* (tes-uh-ree)
A standard mosaic tile term that describes all of the bits and pieces that are applied, with an adhesive, to a base or surface.

Vitreous glass tile is a very popular glass tile that comes in thousands of colors. The tiles have a flat top face and ridged back. Vitreous glass tiles are durable, stain resistant, and a good choice for projects that will brave the elements.

Stained glass comes in thousands of colors, textures, and sizes. Most people remember beautiful stained glass windows adorning houses of worship and cathedrals. Adding stained glass pieces or shards to your projects will provide a magical visual touch that sometimes cannot be captured using anything else. One caveat to working with stained glass is that its thickness doesn't match that of china or tile in most circumstances.

This glass-on-glass project, one of the many projects that can be created using stained glass, won first place in an annual recycled art contest.

Smalti are handmade irregular rectangles of opaque glass in brilliant colors. They have irregular pitted shapes with a very reflective surface.

Ceramic tiles are available in hundreds of colors, sizes, and shapes; they come in glazed or unglazed styles. You can purchase ceramic tile by the piece or by the sheet with either paper or mesh backing.

To remove the paper backing from tile sheets, soak the tile sheet until the paper floats off. Make sure to recycle the paper so you don't clog your drain. Tiles with a mesh backing can be pulled off the backing, or you can glue sections of the tile to your surface with the mesh still attached to the back.

Stones are another interesting addition to a mosaic. You can choose to use polished stones, pebbles, river rocks, marble, granite, or slate. Semi-precious stones, such as turquoise, lapis lazuli, alabaster, quartz, and agate, are also wonderful additions to a mosaic.

Do not attempt to cut stones with basic tile tools. Check with a local tile store or rock shop to seek out assistance in cutting stone.

Everything else
China
Porcelain
Glassware
Seashells
Mother of pearl
Mirror
Colored bottles
Cracked windshield glass
Sea glass
Marbles

The list of materials you can use for tiled projects is almost endless.

More . . .
Glass jewels
Glass gems
Jewelry
Medals
Figurines
Buttons
Game pieces
Keys
Silverware
Wine corks
Small toys

All materials should be free from dirt, grease, and dust. Soak seashells and stones overnight and rinse until the water runs clear.

Basic Tools

Besides a sturdy base, tesserae, and a good adhesive, the only things you'll really need are:

Safety Equipment

- Always wear **safety goggles** when cutting and breaking up tesserae.
- A **dust mask** or **respirator** should be worn when mixing powdered grouts, adhesives, and cements.
- Disposable latex-free **gloves** should be worn when handling grouts, adhesives, and cement products.
- Always read and follow all **safety instructions**.

Cutting Tools

Tile cutters are designed for cutting ceramic tiles, crockery, and china. Better tile nippers have tungsten-carbide cutting edges and spring-loaded handles.

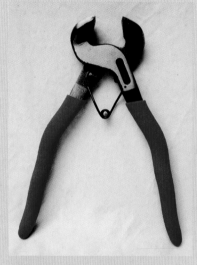

Wheeled glass nippers have a set of wheels on spring-loaded handles. They can be used to cut glass, mirror, glass tiles, and the like, as you would with tile nippers.

Glass cutters, used for cutting and scoring stained glass and mirrors, come in many varieties. My preference is a pistol-grip glass-cutter. You will also need a cork-backed ruler and running pliers, which break the scored glass.

Other Basic Tools

A few other basic tools are always good to have nearby. Many of them are basic household items.
- Wire cutters
- Needle-nose pliers
- Self-closing tweezers are a little more expensive than regular tweezers but well worth the investment. Make sure to keep them glue-free!
- Small hammers are used for breaking large tiles, crockery, glass, mirror, and such into randomly shaped pieces. Ordinary household versions are suitable, but I prefer using a smaller hammer to help control the break.
- Always use an old kitchen towel to cover pieces that you break with a hammer.

- Tools for nipping, pushing, and prodding are handy for moving pieces into place and scraping out excess adhesives, mastic, mortar, or grout. Toothpicks, shish kebab skewers, tweezers, and dental and manicure tools are just some of the options.
- Foam paintbrushes are great for applying sealer before gluing.
- Sandpaper to roughen surfaces.
- Painter's tape to cover delicate areas before grouting.
- For cleanup, keep on hand: newspaper, a roll of paper towels, sponges (look for ones with smaller holes), vinegar, and water.

Adhesive Spreaders

There's not a set way to spread adhesive. It really depends on your personal choice and the adhesives that are being used. Tile floats and trowels of different sizes and types are useful for applying grout, adhesive, and mastic to larger surfaces. For small work, plastic spatulas, butter knives, and palette knives work great. PVA and epoxy adhesives can be applied using small paintbrushes, popsicle sticks, and so on.

Grout Spreader

You may find situations that call for a grout spreader. Again, tile floats come in a variety shapes and sizes and are available at most home improvement stores. For smaller projects, gloved hands usually seem to work best for me!

Shaping and Smoothing Tools

A Dremel tool is a small handheld rotary grinder with multiple bits for grinding and smoothing surfaces. A really great tool to learn how to use, it's available at most home improvement stores.

Power Max II Grinder is a professional grinder that helps to smooth and round out the sharp edges easily.

Adhesives

Many of our visitors to my studio at 225 Water Street think that we create our mosaic tile pieces by embedding objects into wet concrete. While this is a very effective process when making some tiled projects (see page 84), our process for most projects is to prepare the surface, glue the pieces to the surface with the appropriate adhesive, let it dry, grout, and then seal the piece.

To assure success in all of your projects, it's best to read the label and follow the directions from the manufacturer. There is a perfect adhesive out there for every surface. Choosing to just use whatever you have on hand may prove to be a mistake. Pay close attention to your choice of adhesive, especially for outdoor projects. If it's not weatherproof and waterproof, don't use it. Extreme heat and cold can create cracks that may fill with water and dirt, eventually destroying the piece. While there are many to choose from, I stick with the ones that have worked for me.

An **acrylic-based poly vinyl acetate (PVA) adhesive** such as Weldbond is the adhesive of choice for many mosaic tile artists. The reason that I recommend Weldbond adhesive is that through the years I have found it to be the only true PVA adhesive that really does what it says. Weldbond is a nontoxic white glue that dries clear and can pretty much glue anything to everything.

Weldbond can be applied in various ways. You can apply the glue

directly onto the tile, or the surface, from the bottle, or you can "butter" the back of the tile with the adhesive using a popsicle stick.

Although I have found that a PVA adhesive is unmatched as a non-toxic primer for porous surfaces, I wouldn't recommend it when gluing objects that come into contact with water or are exposed to the outdoor elements.

So what is the best adhesive for outdoor projects?

Waterproof adhesives such as Clear Liquid Nails, GE clear Silicone II, Lexel, or E6000 glue, are popular adhesives for projects that may be exposed to water or the outdoors. Again, read the directions carefully to make sure the adhesive you choose meets the needs of your project. Most waterproof adhesives are applied directly from the tube to the piece being glued.

Mastic is a polymer-based adhesive that is spreadable with great "grab," which can be especially important to keep things from sliding. It's a better choice for many indoor/outdoor projects and vertical surfaces. Mastic can be buttered directly onto your pieces and applied to the surface or you can push the pieces into a layer of mastic that has been spread on the surface and forego grouting, in some cases. Mastic can be tinted using pigments in a wide variety of colors. The jury is still out whether mastic is a good choice for outdoor projects. If you've grouted a project that was created using Mastic, make sure to seal the grout to keep moisture from getting underneath the glued pieces.

When in doubt, use . . .

Cement-based mortars or thinset, which are made of cement and silica sand. Thinset is made by mixing the powdered cement with water. You can find quick setting, pre-colored thinset, but I would suggest using products that allow more working time to assure success. Cement-based products are always recommended for most outdoor applications as well as projects that involve concrete or stone surfaces. Always read the directions before using cement-based mortars to make sure that the product will hold up based on outdoor conditions and the surfaces being used.

Epoxy resins are two-part adhesives consisting of a resin and hardener mixed together right before use. Epoxy resins can be used effectively for glass collage or crash glass applications like those made famous by mosaic tile artists Mo Ringey and Ellen Blakely. Epoxy is toxic, so be careful. It can also be somewhat messy, and many brands have varied windows of working opportunity before they set. The amazing mosaic tile artist Laurel Skye recommended Douglas & Sturgess brand (resin #7828 and hardener #8140) in one of her workshops, and that's what I've stuck with. Epoxy resins work great with many materials that don't adhere easily, such as glass and metal.

Whether your projects will survive the test of time will really depend on the adhesive products you've chosen to use. Read and follow the directions with all adhesives and always work in a well-ventilated area.

Color and Theme

Pique assiette mosaic tile is a random display of a myriad of colors and textures. The beauty of the art is your ability to mix and match. The sky is truly the limit!

Color theory is certainly a book within itself. To keep your mosaic tile journey simple, try using a color palette that you tend to gravitate toward. The basic color wheel can help you come up with complementary and contrasting color combinations that are pleasing to the eye.

Use the color wheel to help you choose a complementary color combination or push the envelope using surprising blocks of unexpected color.

Color wheel 101

- Primary colors: red, yellow, and blue
- Secondary colors: green, orange, and purple
- Tertiary colors: yellow-orange, red-orange, red-purple, blue-purple, blue-green, and yellow-green.
- Neutral colors: black, white, tan, and gray.
- Complementary colors are colors that are directly across from each other on the color wheel: red and green, yellow and purple, blue and orange.
- Monochromatic colors are all the color variations (tints, tones, and shades) of a single hue.

If you search the internet for "color wheel" you will find a variety of very useful information that can help guide you with working color combinations. One of my favorite websites to visit for color inspiration is http://www.color matters.com.

Theme and Design

Creative inspiration can come from anywhere—your closet, magazines, home decor, or nature.

The theme you choose is entirely up to you. Designs can range from totally abstract to precisely

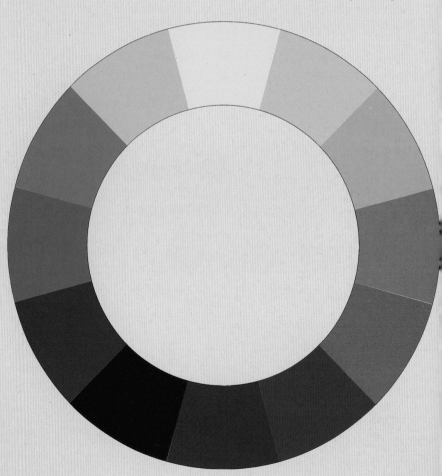

planned. You can copy an existing pattern or create your own design. If you don't want to fly by the seat of your pants, try tracing a pattern from a color book to help guide you in planning the color and movement of the piece.

To keep things simple, break larger designs up into sections so that the project doesn't overwhelm you. Try not to think too much or over plan! Do what makes you feel comfortable. Spontaneity is what's needed to make your design dynamic and interesting.

Go treasure hunting and find cool china plates or a variety of interesting dish patterns first. This will help you establish what colors you should be shooting for. It will also give you an idea of how much more stuff you'll need to finish the piece.

If at first you don't succeed . . .

During our mosaic tile workshops, I let students know that their first mosaic tile project should be about cutting, technique, color, and theme. It's best to not have grandiose expectations, as your first attempt may or may not be to your liking. As you start down the tiled path, keep this in mind: if you don't like what you've glued or what you've glue stuff to, you can always start over. Don't let fear stop you from trying. It's just stuff! Most of it would otherwise end up in a drawer, basement, garage, or, worse yet, a landfill. Always try to remind yourself that it's never over until you grout. My suggestion is to go with your first thought and glue it down. If you don't like it, that's what needle-nose pliers are for!

Selecting a Base

"An idea that is developed and put into action is more important than an idea that exists only as an idea." —Edward de Bono

You can glue found objects to nearly any surface. Selecting the base material becomes a matter of shape, function, and personal taste.

When selecting a base, think about the following:
- Is the surface strong enough to hold the combined weight of the objects and grout?
- Do you have the correct adhesive to attach the bits and pieces to the base?

Commonly Used Base Materials

Wood can be cut to any shape and size, making it ideal for many indoor projects. You can create a mosaic project on any wood surface, but be aware that plywood is not a waterproof base and can (and will) expand, contract, sag, or warp, especially if exposed to the elements on a continual basis. Using high-grade plywood (at least 3/4 inch thick) will provide a rigid support and help counteract warping, but you may want to use alternatives, such as HardieBacker or concrete backer board (available at home centers), just to be safe. As with most bases, you will want to roughen the surface a bit before gluing the objects.

    Terracotta and clay objects offer a wide variety of shapes and

sizes to create mosaics on. Before gluing, seal the object with a water-based polyurethane or coat of PVA adhesive. Let dry completely before tiling.

You can add bits and pieces to **concrete** objects like birdbaths, stepping-stones, and planters. Make sure you use the proper adhesive—mastic, cement-based mortars, or silicone. Remember to cut your pieces small enough to lie flat, especially on rounded surfaces. Reseal the piece with grout sealer once a year if the piece is exposed to the elements or water.

You can glue bits and pieces on **glass**: windows (new or old) or glass objects like bowls and vases. Glass surfaces should always be prepared before gluing. Brush a coat of Weldbond onto those slippery surfaces and let it dry. This technique helps provide that "tooth" needed to hold the tiles in place. You'll want to have some painter's tape nearby, to hold the pieces in place if they keep sliding. Patience is an important virtue for mosaic artists. If you have no patience for slipping and sliding, use mastic.

Mesh netting is the netting that is found on the backs of many sheets of ceramic tile. It can be purchased in rolls and is easily cut to any size or shape. The tile is glued to the netting, the excess is trimmed, and the whole thing is then glued onto the permanent base in manageable sections. Applying tile to mesh netting is a great way to do a beginner backsplash project without worrying about things slipping and sliding.

When gluing objects to a mesh backing, remember to protect your work surface so you don't glue the mesh to it.

Walls, fixtures, plaster items, ceramics, containers, trays, and other found objects can also be used as bases—use your imagination!

Surface preparation
Once you've chosen your base, you need to prepare the surface. Base surfaces should be clean, dry, and free from rust or chipping paint. When applying objects to interior/exterior walls, make sure to score the surface with sharp knife or gently sand the surface to improve the adhesion of objects. Seal porous surfaces like wood and terracotta by brushing on a diluted solution of PVA adhesive to prevent the tiles from being dislodged by the water.

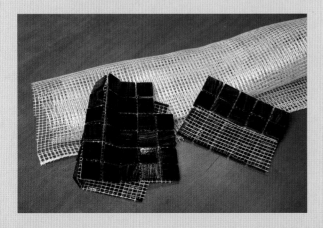

Basic Cutting Techniques

"Happiness lies in the joy of achievement and the thrill of creative effort."
—Franklin Roosevelt

Getting comfortable with cutting tiles, china, glass, and found objects takes time. The more you practice, the more accurate you become. *Always wear safety glasses when cutting tile, china, or glass.*

Cutting ceramic tiles

Preferred tool(s): tile cutter or wheeled glass nipper

Ceramic tiles that are manageable sizes can be hand-cut into smaller uniform or random pieces. If you are cutting larger ceramic tiles, I would suggest having them cut with a wet saw if you need them perfectly straight. Most home improvement stores and local tile centers charge a minimal fee to cut tile using their wet saw.

The consensus is that the tile cutter is the best tool for cutting ceramic tiles. However, many mosaic tile artists, including me, prefer to use the wheeled glass nipper instead. But don't let that stop you from practicing with a tile cutter. You never know until you try. It really depends on your hand strength.

Start by putting on your safety glasses. The rule of thumb is to cut against the ridges on the backs of ceramic tiles. Angle the tile cutter blades onto the tile in the direction you want the cut to go. Hold the tile securely with your index finger and thumb. For half cuts and diagonals, place the blades about 1/3 of the way onto the tile, and squeeze the cutter quickly.

Tile Tip

Attempting to cut ceramic tiles dead center with tile cutters can prove to be an impossible task.

If you're not getting straight edges, keep trying. But remember that uneven cuts and weird edges are used quite successfully in mosaic tile and found object pieces.

Cutting stone and rock is a completely different story and is not considered a basic technique. If you're lucky enough to have a rock store in the area, these would be the folks to talk to about cutting rock and stone. If not, check with a local home improvement or tile store.

Cutting glass tiles

Preferred tool: wheeled glass nipper

Cutting vitreous glass and stained glass tiles in halves, quarters, small squares, and triangles takes practice. Using your thumb and forefinger can help you position the tile for better accuracy with straight and diagonal cuts. As when cutting ceramic tiles, hold the tile firmly and point the cutter in the direction you want the cut to go. Once you've found the spot, hold the tile firmly. Pop the wheeled glass nipper quickly. Practice makes perfect.

Cutting porcelain figurines

Suggested tool(s): wheeled glass nipper, tile cutter, or small hammer (depends)

Cutting porcelain figurines and floral treasures has a life of its own. The beauty of this art form is its forgiveness for what may be considered mistakes.

If you're expecting perfection, practice and then practice some more.

Sometimes you can grab onto certain areas of a figurine to attempt to remove desired parts with the wheeled glass nippers. If that doesn't work, try the tile cutter, in certain circumstances.

If you're not feeling comfortable with the cutting tools, grab a small hammer, safety glasses, and an old dish towel.

Protect your work table before using a hammer on objects, and wear safety glasses. Always cover the piece to be broken with a dish towel. Grip the area

Hammer Tip

Tap firmly. Don't smash.

of the piece you want to remove. Holding the object firmly, tap the piece with the hammer, a little to the side of the area you are trying to remove. It's trial and error. A little prayer and practice go a long way.

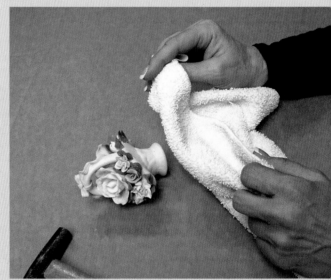

I've found that removing flowers from vintage knick-knacks is sometimes easier than it looks. Many of these lovely treasures were cast with hollow centers, giving you the option of removing each flower separately with wheeled glass nippers. That is, of course, if you can get the wheels around the pieces.

Hand cutting china

A golf instructor once directed me to visualize the shot in my mind and see the ball landing on the green. I use that same routine when hand-cutting china. Holding the china firmly, I envision the cut that the wheeled glass nippers will make. This may sound silly, but it works more often than not. Sometimes, of course, it's just pure luck.

China Anatomy

- **Border: the ring around the plate or cup, the edge**
- **Center: the middle of the plate, which I like to call a medallion**
- **Signature: the maker of the plate (found on the back)**
- **Footprint: the ring on the bottom of the plate, the part in contact with the table**

China Tip

Try to select plates with smaller footprints. Plates with larger footprints offer less material to work with, so take that into account when you're selecting a pattern. Personally, I have a tough time throwing anything away, so I have a huge box of china footprints. Many will reside in my garden forevermore.

While there are various ways, which you will discover through trial and error, to preserve key areas while cutting a china plate or cup, I've had some success maintaining the centers by starting to cut about a third of the way down the plate, instead of dead center. I have found that this approach increases the odds of keeping the center of the plate somewhat intact.

Once you remove the borders of the plate, begin to cut border pieces into the sizes you want. Border pieces don't have to be exactly perfect. It all depends on your comfort level. Remember that you want the pieces to lie flat. If your cut china pieces don't lie flat, cutting them a little bit smaller will flatten them out.

Cup handles

If you're trying to remove cup handles or specific parts of a piece, it's best to make the first cut with the wheeled glass nippers. The odds of success are much greater when removing a desired area if you start the cut a little further away from the area that you want to remove.

Once you have removed the piece, carefully begin cutting and shaping to the desired size. Smooth it out to the best of your ability, hopefully keeping the piece intact. Remember, you can always glue it back together, if you mess up.

Be aware that when working with cups, vases, and other glass objects, you win some and you lose some. It's not an exact science. If it's an heirloom and you don't feel comfortable cutting the piece, don't. There are plenty of other cool things you can, and should, practice on. The object of the craft is to have fun—I don't want you to feel sick or start crying if a cut goes awry!

When in doubt, don't. Just put the nippers down, and step away slowly!

Putting the pieces back together

So, now you're energized to get right on to that mosaic tile patio table with the place settings embedded into it. It's the one mosaic tile project that everyone always asks me about. Not the easiest beginner project to take on, but hey, it could happen!

One of the easiest ways I have found to keep the pieces of a broken plate intact is to use contact paper. There are mosaic tile adhesive sheets that you can purchase, but contact paper is cheaper and easier to find.

Gluing a broken plate back together works best if you have chosen a plate that has a small footprint. A small footprint makes it a whole lot easier to recreate a plate that lies flat, when it's glued back together. Large footprints can be used but it takes more time to position the pieces back into a mostly flat design.

Protect your worktable before breaking the plates. Cut a piece of the contact paper large enough to cover the plate, then peel off the backing and attach the sticky side to the front of the plate. Work the contact paper onto the plate so that it's secure. Turn the plate over so the back is facing you. Cover the plate with a dish towel and put on your safety glasses.

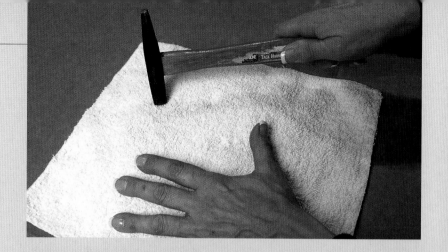

Take a small hammer and firmly tap the dish. Don't smash—larger pieces are easier to put back together. A lot depends on where you make the first blow. Sometimes if you go right for the middle you end up with too many tiny pieces. That's why practicing with pieces that you don't cherish is a good idea. Once you're comfortable with the outcomes you've experienced, move on to try your hand at cutting more treasured items.

You can lift the towel to check your work. If you still need to break more of the plate, cover it with the towel and continue tapping with the hammer until you are happy with the pieces. Remove the towel and turn the plate over. Most of the plate pieces should be stuck directly to the contact paper—unless, of course, you've used the plate as a stress reliever.

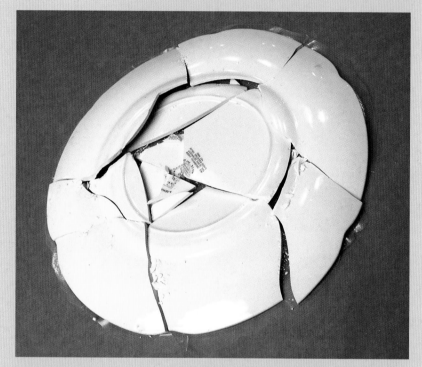

Now that you have the entire plate, broken but mostly intact, you can begin to rebuild the plate piece by piece. This process is slow but sure. Take the extra time needed to make sure that all the pieces lie flat.

Arranging the Pieces

"One of the advantages of being disorderly is that one is constantly making exciting discoveries." —A. A. Milne

You've found your base. You have your materials. Now what?

Play with different combinations of your found objects. Place them on your surface to see how they look and work together. Experiment, stand back, look, rearrange, change, and stand back again until you're satisfied. Do what you like and don't be afraid to change your mind as the project unfolds. It's never over—until you've grouted!

Pique assiette mosaics can be very stimulating to the viewer. When laying out the bits and pieces, try to remember that the eye will mix the shapes and colors. Here are some ways you can make your composition more interesting:

■ Vary the size and shape of pieces as they meet each other.

- Think odd numbers, as in flower arrangements. Mix pieces of opposite colors together for contrast.
- Instead of covering a large area with the same tile, vary the shades you are using to add interest (unless of course, the effect you want is a uniform block of color).

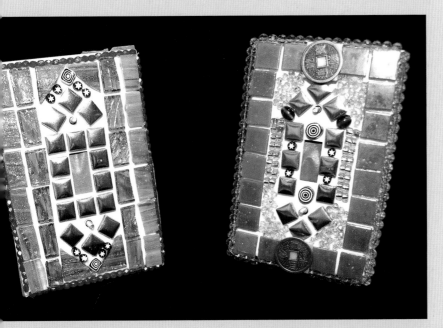

Think about how the shards will play off each other. Try to keep in mind that the piece will look completely different once it's grouted. As the project unfolds, you will have a better idea of the grout color that would enhance the piece. Choosing a grout color is a trial-and-error process. If you choose a grout color that is similar to the pieces you've glued, they may disappear. Mosaic tile artists usually suggest grout colors in the black, gray, beige, and brown families.

The sky's the limit!

Grouting Your Project

Grout is a cement-based material (like mortar, but made with a much finer sand) that is used to fill in the gaps between glued tiles and found objects. There are hundreds of colors to choose from; I find that many of the colors I choose are readily available in powdered form. You can mix your own grout colors, if you want to, by adding grout pigments or artist's acrylics. Experimenting is always good. Just make sure to whip up enough of your custom color the first time. Somehow, you never can quite come up with the same color twice.

Grout color is a matter of personal preference and will completely change the final look of your project. The best choices include dark gray, shades of dark brown, off-white, and black. Keep in mind that a grout color that is very similar to the object colors will blend with the design and may not give you the "pop" you're looking for.

Fact: Grout can be up to two shades darker when wet.

An Important Grout Rule

Do not allow grout, wet or dry, to come in contact with drains or commodes.

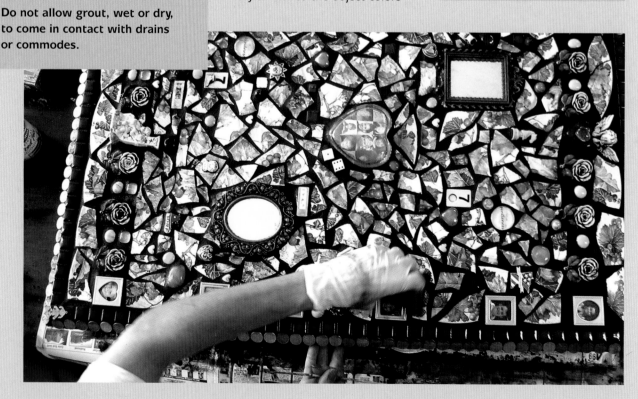

There are two types of grout: sanded and unsanded.

- Sanded grout is best used for tile projects with 1/8-inch or larger gaps.
- Unsanded grout is suggested for gaps smaller than 1/8 inch.

You'll find premixed grout-adhesive combination products at your local home improvement store. While they look appealing, a way to save time and money, I do not recommend these products. They are great as an adhesive but a real mess to grout with. However, I do recommend mixing your grout with a latex additive in lieu of water, for more flexibility.

Grout can be mixed in a variety of bowls, buckets, old cans, and Ziploc bags. I prefer to mix smaller quantities of grout in Ziploc bags. It's so much easier to thoroughly mix, keep wet, and dispose of! Mixed grout cannot be reused.

Gloves and a facemask should always be worn when mixing powdered grout.

Grout should be mixed with water or a grout additive to a consistency close to that of peanut butter and not quite that of oatmeal.

Leftover grout should never be washed down any drain or emptied into a water source. This can prove to be a very costly mistake. Grout can be disposed of in your regular garbage.

A little bit of pre-grouting advice: it's best to get into the habit of protecting all delicate areas that shouldn't be exposed to grout, such as jewelry, metals, wood pieces, pearls, and the like. Painter's tape (blue masking tape) seems to be the easiest solution. It just takes a few minutes and is certainly worth the extra time you save in cleanup alone. Plus, you'll be protecting precious metals, wood, and beautiful jewels from being permanently discolored. It's better to be safe than sorry. You'll be glad you did!

Mixing Grout

1. Scoop about 1½ to 2 cups of grout into a plastic bag.
2. Start by adding small amounts of water and blend.
3. Knead the grout to moisten. Make sure to shake down the corners.
4. Add water by the tablespoon, as needed. Grout too wet? Add a little more grout.
5. Keep kneading. Add water as needed.
6. When the grout has reached a "almost peanut butter, not quite oatmeal" consistency, let it set up for a minute or two.
7. Knead it again and you're ready to start grouting!

Grouting Your Project

You should always wear gloves when applying grout.
1. Take a handful of grout and start to push it gently into the gaps of your piece.
2. Keep filling gaps, smoothing as you go.
3. Don't get carried away. Just cover the pieces with grout, making sure that all of the cracks and crevices are filled.
4. Build up the grout around extruded objects for a more secure hold.

> **If your grout starts to crumble, don't add more water—it may crack when dry. Mix a new batch and start again.**

5. Smaller projects can be grouted completely before removing grout. Larger projects should be grouted in sections to help keep cleanup somewhat easier. The drier the grout, the harder you have to work to get it off.
6. Once the project is covered with grout and all gaps have been filled, grab a roll of paper towels and rip off a few sheets to start the cleanup.
7. Start rubbing the excess grout away from the surface with the paper towel. Use a new paper towel as often as you need one.

8. Keep wiping, cleaning, and removing excess grout. You will eventually get it all off.

> If an object that you have glued becomes dislodged during the grouting process, remove it. Clean the excess grout from the piece and the area. Wait until you've finished grouting to try to repair that area. Grab your adhesive and glue the object back in place. Grout is not an adhesive, so don't skip the glue. Let it set up for a short time, then carefully, using the same grout as before, push it gently into the repaired area. Be careful. Don't fuss with it. Just let it be. Patience!

9. You can use a wooden skewer or other pointed object to remove additional grout around the piece, exposing more of the item. This is a matter of personal choice and should be a gentle process that is best done with, again, patience.
10. Keep smoothing, pressing, and wiping.
11. Inspect the piece to make sure that all of the crevices, holes, and gaps have been filled. If not, press a little more grout into those areas. Smooth and clean.
12. When the piece is clean and you are satisfied that everything has been uncovered, remove the painter's tape from the delicate areas and let the grout dry.
13. Mix equal parts vinegar and water. *Dampen, don't soak,* a paper towel or soft sponge. Carefully start to clean off the grout haze that may have developed.
14. Let the piece set up a bit. Continue to wipe down with the vinegar and water mixture every so often. The grout will eventually settle and stop shedding.
15. Grout appears to be dry in a few hours but it can take up to three days to completely dry. This really depends on the environment and the size of the project.

For projects used in a functional capacity, or outdoors, it's recommended that the grout be sealed with a silicone sealant when completely dry, to prevent moisture from getting in and staining the project.

16. Any sharp edges that remain should be smoothed with a Dremel tool after the grout has completely dried.

Projects

Switch Plate Covers

Whenever I get the itch to redecorate a room I always find myself in search of cool switch plate covers. But standing in electrical departments looking for unique examples of these got really old, really fast. Once in a while—and I mean once in a very long while—I'd get lucky and find a fantastic cover that I just had to have. Unfortunately, those rare finds were not worth the time I spent looking for them—especially when I could be busy making my own.

Creating custom switch plate covers is a project that anyone can do, and the creative combinations are endless. Hard to imagine that you can take a 49-cent plastic switch plate cover and turn it into a work of art? Well, I'm about to make a believer out of you.

As you start this project, keep a few things in mind:

- Pieces to be glued must be free of any sharp edges and should lie as flat as possible.
- Keep the middle switch area and screw holes open, so that the switch plate can be attached to the wall and function.
- Make sure that the back of the switch plate is clean and free of grout.

Materials

For each of the projects in this book, I've included a materials list to give you a better idea of the amount of materials you will need to complete a project of this size. China patterns and additional elements will vary, based on your findings, with every project.

- Hard plastic switch plate covers—singles or doubles. Metal and wood ones can also be used.
- Funky china
- Jewelry, millefiori, beads, tiles, marbles, and mirror
- Sanded grout (charcoal)

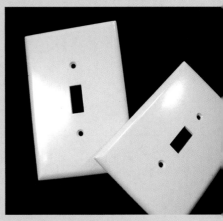

Tools

- Wheeled glass nipper
- Tile cutter
- Safety glasses
- Paintbrush or foam brush
- PVA (Weldbond) adhesive was used for this project, but mastic can also be used
- Roll of painter's tape
- Disposable latex-free gloves
- Large Ziploc bag
- Paper towels
- Q-tips, skewers, toothpicks, or small tools for prodding and cleaning
- Vinegar and water

Directions

1. Cover your workspace with newspaper.
2. Coat the switch plate cover with Weldbond. Let it dry completely.
3. With the wheeled glass nipper, cut china, tile, and mirror pieces to desired sizes. Again, be sure that all of the pieces lie flat and have no sharp edges.
4. Glue smaller items, such as beads or tiles, around the switch opening(s) to begin.

5. I prefer to start gluing the inner and outer edges of a switch-plate first. It helps me determine how much space I'll have left for the remaining materials that complete the piece. Use painter's tape to secure an object that may start to slide.

6. When working on the outer edge make sure to glue your pieces on the flat part of the outer edge of the switch plate. If you try to attach pieces to the rounded edge, you'll have a difficult time getting them to stick. Remember, you're going to grout this, and after it's up on the wall you won't see the rounded edge.

7. Fill in the rest of the open areas of your switch plate with tiles, china, glass, and objects of the same thickness, gluing as you go.

8. Check that pieces are securely glued and free from excess adhesive. Let everything dry for a minimum of 24 hours before grouting.

9. Make sure that the screw holes and switch openings are covered or marked, so you can clean them easily after grouting.

10. Remember to protect delicate objects from grout with painter's tape before you begin the grouting process.

5

8

Gluing Beads

I used beads on a few of the examples. Beads can be glued independently, or you can create a string of beads if they aren't already strung. Knot one end of the string, then string enough beads to fill the area you want beaded. Finish by knotting the loose end to keep the beads tight and securely in place. With your glue bottle, lay down a nice strip of glue on the area to be beaded. No need to get carried away—use just enough glue to set the beads into.

Take the beaded string and carefully lay it into the glue. It's okay if the string beyond the knot sticks out; you can cut it off after the glue dries, before grouting.

11. Grout the switch plate and clean.
12. Let dry for 24 hours.
13. Polish.
14. You may need to purchase longer screws to attach the switch plate to the wall. These can be found at any hardware or home improvement store.

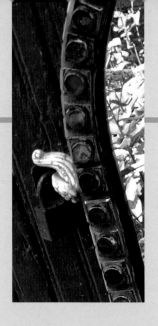

One Man's Trash

"To invent, you need a good imagination and a pile of junk." —Thomas Edison

The most delightful—but frightening—phone calls I receive are from people in my life who know about my addiction to stuff. All I have to hear is, "We're moving soon, do you want to stop over and take a peek at our junk before we take it to the Goodwill?"

Hmm. Let me think. I'm lucky if the phone makes it back onto the base before I'm out the door.

This project was completed using a mirror that my daughter discarded as junk before she moved. A couple of things attracted me to the piece: it was heavy, it hangs on the wall, and the frame is wide enough to glue something to it.

As it happened, once again, the mirror turned into another great project with little or no cutting.

While I was collecting materials for this piece, I thought about where the mirror would find a home, once completed. Eventually, I settled on a Zen theme, wanting to use some of the Japanese china, coins, and small Buddha figurines that I have collected over the years. Why Buddhas? They're happy and peaceful.

The mirror's border measures a little over 1 inch, and it is very easy to find ready-made precut tiles in 3/4-inch and 1-inch sizes. Precut tiles in ceramic, glass, and mirror come in a myriad of colors and sizes, so it's usually easy to find just the right one for your project. Iridescent glass tiles are a favorite of mine, especially after they've been grouted!

Materials

- Hand-me-down mirror
- Paint
- Buddha figurine
- Japanese coins
- One sheet (144 tiles) of 1-inch iridescent glass tiles (cherry red)
- One pound 3/4-inch iridescent glass chips (pink)
- One sheet (208 rounds) of iridescent rounds (cherry red)
- Rice bowls and two sauce bowls
- Carved place card holders
- Variety of old jewelry
- Sanded grout (charcoal)

Tools

- Wheeled glass nipper
- Tile cutter
- Safety glasses
- Paintbrush or foam brush
- Sandpaper
- PVA (Weldbond) adhesive was used for this project, but mastic can also be used
- Roll of painter's tape
- Disposable latex-free gloves
- Large Ziploc bag
- Paper towels
- Q-tips, skewers, toothpicks, or small tools for prodding and cleaning
- Vinegar and water

If I Had It to Do Over Again

I would have painted the frame of the mirror a lighter color, knowing that I was using a darker iridescent tile. The completed piece didn't quite pop the way I wanted it to. The upside, of course, is that it blends.

Directions

1. Cover your workspace with newspaper.
2. Clean the mirror and cover it with newspaper, using painter's tape to secure.
3. Clean the border of the mirror with a vinegar and water mixture. Let it dry.
4. If you want to paint the border, do so now and let it dry completely. Keep in mind that post-grout touch-ups may be needed, so save some paint.
5. When the paint is dry, lightly coat the frame with Weldbond and a foam brush. Let dry. Make sure you don't glue it to your work table.
6. With the wheeled glass nippers, remove the desired sections from the bowls and saucers. Shape the pieces so that they will fit and lie somewhat flat on the frame. Set aside.

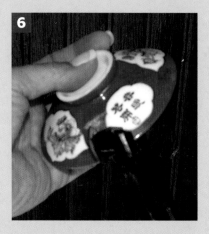

7. The cherry-red glass tiles and rounds come on a paper backing. Soak the paper off the back of the tiles in the sink. Let them sit until the paper starts floating. Gather the paper from the sink and recycle it. Don't let it go down the drain! Get a colander and gather the tiles from the sink. Let them dry thoroughly before gluing.

Sheets of Tile

If you're using tiles with mesh backing, you can pull the tiles off the mesh before gluing or cut around the tiles, preserving the mesh for extra hold.

8. Glue the 1-inch red tiles evenly along the bottom edge of the mirror, leaving about a 1/4- to 1/2-inch space in between each pair of tiles.
9. Remove the pin back from the Buddha pin and glue it dead center on the frame to round out the design.
10. Take two of the rounded china pieces from one of the saucers and glue one to each of the bottom corners of the mirror.
11. Next, glue the 1-inch tiles evenly around the entire mirror border, leaving about a 1/4- to 1/2-inch space in between each pair of tiles. If there is excess adhesive peeking out from behind the tiles, let it set up a bit before cleaning it out with a wooden skewer and a paper towel. Let the adhesive dry.

12. Once the 1-inch red tiles are fairly dry, you can add a little depth by gluing a round red glass tile to the top of each of the square glass tiles. The different geometric shapes really play well off of each other.

13. While the mirror is still lying flat, attach the four ivory place card holders onto the sides of the mirror and secure them with painter's tape. These cool found objects will provide a few places to hang scarves and so on.

14. Now is a great time to attach the pink iridescent stained glass tiles to the sides. It's a slow but worthwhile process. Gather a little patience and make sure to check your work from time to time. Pieces have a tendency to slide, so check back often while the pieces are drying. It's a lot easier to adjust things that are still moveable than to attempt a complete do-over.

15. Attach the Buddha figurine to the top of the mirror and use painter's tape to secure it.

16. Once the tiles are firmly set, layer coins or jewelry on top of them, as desired.

A Time Saver

Pay attention to the direction you glue certain pieces in. There may very well be a right way and a wrong way. It really pays off if you want certain tiles or objects to serve a purpose, such as a place to hang things.

17. Let the finished piece dry for a minimum of 24 hours.
18. Tape off the areas you want protected from the grout.
19. Grout the project. Clean, hang, and enjoy!

Cat Nap

"Creativity is the quality that you bring to the activity that you are doing. It is an attitude, an inner approach—how you look at things . . . Whatsoever you do, if you do it joyfully, if you do it lovingly, if your act of doing is not purely economical, then it is creative." —Osho

Catalyst for this project: Two black and white cat figurines procured from a thrift store.

The Cat Nap project is the first in a series of three basic picture frame projects, which concentrate on the technique of hand-cutting china. These 8-by-8–inch picture frame projects were selected to help you concentrate on basic cutting techniques, using different china patterns and glass objects.

Yes, you can break a plate—under a towel—with a hammer, but while therapeutic, it's not the most precise method. When you want to control the break, use a wheeled glass nipper for the best results. See the Cutting chapter for detailed information on how to cut your china they way you want it.

Cutting tile and china takes practice. The more you cut, the better you get at it. One of the perks of pique assiette is that you don't have to have straight, smooth edges unless you really want to. It's supposed to look funky. If you ask me (which I'm going to assume you just did, since you're reading this book), the imperfect nature of this whimsical craft is one of its most appealing aspects.

It really is all it's cracked up to be (slight pun intended). Have fun!

Materials

- 8-by-8-by-$^3/_4$–inch basic wooden picture frame. Precut craft frames and assorted wooden shapes are available at some craft stores, but mostly online. Kudos to you if you have a family member that has a table saw and knows how to use it.

- Paint color of your choice (if you plan on painting the raw wood)
- Black and white cat figurine
- Small dessert plate with a funky border
- One hundred (fifty of each color) 3/4-inch black and white ceramic tiles
- Eight flat-bottomed gems (four red, four blue)
- Twenty 1/2-inch tapestry mirror tiles (gold)
- Assorted millefiori (black)
- Thirty-two pearlescent glass 3/4-inch tiles
- Thirty-six cobalt glass 5/8-inch tiles
- Four 3/4-inch ceramic circles (black)
- Clear glass heart with de-coupage image
- Sanded grout (charcoal)

Tools
- Wheeled glass nipper
- Tile cutter
- Safety glasses
- Paintbrush or foam brush to paint frame
- Sandpaper
- PVA (Weldbond) adhesive was used for this project, but mastic can also be used
- Roll of painter's tape
- Disposable latex-free gloves
- Large Ziploc bag
- Paper towels
- Q-tips, skewers, toothpicks, or small tools for prodding and cleaning
- Mirror insert (if it didn't come with the frame)
- Vinegar and water

Directions

1. Cover your workspace with newspaper.
2. If you want to paint the raw wood, do it now and let it dry completely. Keep a little extra paint for any touch-ups that may be needed after grouting.
3. When dry, lightly sand the frame in all of the places where pieces will be glued.
4. With the wheeled glass nipper, remove the border from the china plate. You'll notice that we didn't have to worry about preserving the center of this plate so cutting it in half right across the middle was the best way to start removing the border of the plate easily.

Tip

If the cut dishware pieces don't lie flat, cut them smaller.

5. Butter the backs of the black and white ceramic tiles with adhesive and start to glue them around the outer border of the frame. Leave at least 1/8-inch in between each tile for the grout line.

Tip

Starting with the outer border on this project helps to give you a guide to follow while filling in the rest of the frame. If you start gluing the inner and outer edges first, you won't have to guess how much room you'll have left to fill.

6. Glue the plate border around the mirror opening. Be sure to leave enough room at each corner to glue the black round ceramic circles into place.

7. Attach the 3/8-inch iridescent glass dark blue tile next, leaving a space once again at each corner to glue the four flat gems.
8. Cut a corner off of two pearlescent tiles. Working your way to the inside of the frame, glue the 3/4-inch pearlescent glass tiles, again leaving a space in each corner to attach the red flat gems. Use the two cut tiles to border the glass heart on the bottom row.
9. Fill any empty space around the black ceramic circles with assorted millefiori.
10. Glue one gold tapestry mirrored tile on top of each one of the white ceramic tiles around the outside border for contrast. Layering tiles adds interest and is always a unique option to center the piece.
11. Once you've glued all of your pieces into place, let the glue set for at least 30 minutes or

Extruded Objects

The cat in this project is extruded, meaning it sticks out further than everything else. Weldbond has been known to hold larger objects into place quite well, although mastic is a better choice in certain circumstances. The following picture frame projects are non-functioning mosaic tile pieces; they won't experience constant use, so Weldbond will work just fine. In more advanced and larger projects, oddly shaped pieces should be embedded into mastic for a much stronger hold.

more before attaching the final cat figurine.

13. Butter the glue or mastic onto the back of the entire figurine. Don't get carried away with the amount of adhesive being used. You really don't want to have excess glue (or mastic) seeping out from underneath set objects. If you do have excess peeking out, let it set up for a bit to make the cleanup easier. I prefer using a wooden skewer and a paper towel for cleaning up wayward adhesive.

14. Carefully glue the cat figurine directly on top of the semi-dry tiles, just above the picture/mirror opening at dead center. Check that pieces are securely glued and free from excess adhesive. Let everything dry for a minimum of 24 hours before grouting.

15. Remember to protect delicate objects and painted areas with painter's tape before you begin the grouting process. Grout the picture frame, building up a layer of grout around any large objects, such as the figurine, to secure them. Clean and polish the frame, then insert a mirror or picture.

That's Not Old Blue Willow!

One of my early mosaic tile projects was a wooden key holder. I intended to decorate this little treasure with a piece of Old Willow china that I found at a garage sale. At the last minute, I added a little Buddha figurine that my dad had bought me while he was in Hawaii with my mom, years earlier. With only two objects and a little glue, I was able to create a very simple, yet functional, piece.

Never aspiring to be an expert collector of china for any other purpose than to break it, I didn't give the china pattern a second thought.

Not long after, that finished piece was displayed as a sample in an art fair, and I found myself being scolded by an antique collector. She let it be known (in a very abrasive manner) that breaking a plate of that value was unheard of. She said the plate was worth at least thirty dollars; what in the world I was thinking? I wasn't. I loved the china. I broke it. I glued and grouted it. And the best part is, I still use this key hanger. It's displayed prominently in my hallway, and it actually holds my keys. In fact, it receives more use, admiration, and attention than it ever would have in its previous incarnation as a solitary, mismatched plate.

That simple piece, created with a chipped Old Willow plate, lets me begin my day remembering my dad with a smile. It never fails.

The point is that you will run across amazing treasures on this journey called pique assiette. You'll never look at castoffs in quite the same way. Objects that you would never imagine being interested in will suddenly jump off the shelves at thrift stores, Goodwill stores, and garage sales.

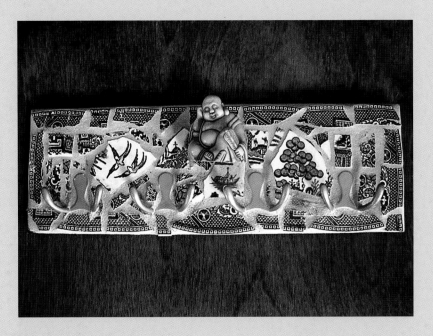

Dumpster diving outings may become a way of life (just a friendly warning). Nothing will be safe from you and your glue.

But there may come a time when you have to decide if the treasures you have found are those that truly inspire you to create that perfect mosaic tile piece—or if they are better left unbroken. You might choose to take a minute to research your find on a website such as replacements.com. It's worth checking out the value of an object, especially if you plan on selling your artwork.

I tend to follow this rule: if I love it, I break it and glue it to something. But in all honesty, there are pieces that I can't bring myself to break—or sell. When I find myself questioning the value of certain things, I do take the time to research them. And that's an exciting adventure in itself— kind of like my own little version of the *Antiques Roadshow*.

So once again, I've crossed a line that tends to disturb many antique collectors and broken up another piece of Old Willow china. This familiar, friendly, and often-mimicked historical pattern is always a favorite. It's pretty easy to find the copycats or even the real thing while thrifting for your next kitschy blue plate special.

If you want to know the value of the Old Willow dessert plates that I used for this project, you'll have to look them up yourself. I already did, and I've had to let go of that balloon.

When you start collecting china, over time you'll acquire a new appreciation for the cool patterns that have graced people's homes. Every piece truly tells a story. Just think about all the happy, awkward, or dramatic family events your china has witnessed!

It's a good day when you're treasure hunting and you stumble upon unique china patterns and dishware. Bonus days are those that bless you with multiple pieces that are laden with amazing borders, full plate designs, centers, and signature backs.

This project is a great way to get comfortable with cutting china borders, china centers, and china signatures.

Now, it's your turn. Gather your wheeled glass nipper and the china. Keep in mind that you want to preserve the outside border, the center medallion of the plate, and the signature on the backside from one of the plates.

Tip

When a cut doesn't go as planned and an unfortunate break occurs, just remember that you can glue it back together. The more you practice, the less frustration you'll experience.

Materials

- 8-by-8-by-3/4–inch basic wooden picture frame. Precut craft frames and assorted wooden shapes are available at some craft stores, but mainly online.
- Paint color of your choice, if you plan on painting the raw wood
- Two Old Willow dessert plates (full design)
- Fifty 3/4-inch ceramic tiles (cobalt blue)
- Four bronze glass gems (flat bottom)
- Four 1/2-inch gold tapestry mirror tiles
- Assorted red millefiori
- Sanded grout (almond color)
- Mirror or glass insert (if it didn't come with the frame)

Tools

- Wheeled glass nipper
- Tile cutter
- Safety glasses
- Paintbrush or foam brush
- Sandpaper
- PVA (Weldbond) adhesive was used for this project, but mastic can also be used
- Roll of painter's tape
- Disposable latex-free gloves
- Large ziploc bag
- Paper towels
- Q-tips, skewers, toothpicks, or small tools for prodding and cleaning
- Vinegar and water

Directions

1. Cover your workspace with newspaper.
2. If you want to paint the raw wood, do it now and let it dry completely. Keep a little extra paint for any touch-ups that may be needed after grouting.
3. When it's dry, lightly sand the frame in all of the places where pieces will be glued.
4. Cut your materials into desired pieces, preserving the borders, a signature, and a medalion.
5. Take sixteen ceramic tiles of equal size and create a square of four in each corner of the frame.
6. Glue the remaining ceramic tiles to the outside border of the picture frame. Keep the spacing equal between each tile. Feel free to move tiles around to get them to fit. Step back for a moment to get a feel for the balance of the piece, and even things out if necessary.
7. Glue the precut china border around the picture/mirror opening.

8. Attach the precut china signature from the back of one of the plates and glue it into the middle of the frame, top center.

9. Place the precut china center medallion of the plate, in the bottom center of the frame.

10. Fill the rest of the frame with the remaining china shards. Cut them smaller as needed.

11. Glue a gold tapestry mirror to each bronze glass gem. Set aside to dry. Glue a gem in each corner.

12. Add any finishing touches. I added a few pieces of millefiori here and there.

13. Clean off any excess adhesive. Let the piece dry for a minimum of 24 hours. When dry, apply painter's tape to areas that you don't want exposed to grout.

Grout Lines

An amazing visual transformation takes place in your piece when it's grouted. Grout color and the thickness of grout lines have a major effect on how a piece looks. Decide ahead of time whether you want your bits and pieces to blend with the grout color, or choose to go with a darker shade to really make the pieces pop.

Darker grout shades tend to be favored by many mosaic tile artists, and with good reason. It's like basic black in your wardrobe. It's slimming, tasteful, and looks good on just about anybody. My advice is to glue the shards closer together and grout with a color on the darker side of the spectrum.

Some of the projects in this book have been intentionally grouted with a questionable choice of grout color. As you can see in the Old Willow picture frame, I feel that the shards could have been closer together and a darker grout shade would have given the shards center stage. Again, it's very much a personal choice.

14. Grout your project. Clean the frame, let it dry, and polish.
15. Insert a mirror or photo.

Oh, Baby!

Catalyst for this project: vintage floral baby vase

The "Oh, Baby!" frame is the final project in our basic picture frame series. This project will help you get more comfortable with removing specific areas from cups and oddly shaped found objects. Many of the same cutting principles you've already learned apply in this technique.

In this project, I could have cut the baby, duck, and flower pieces in half to make them lie flat. As you can see from the finished piece, I decided not to.

If, like me, you want to take the 3D route (for lack of a better term), instead of the "cut it until it lays flat" option, pay special attention to making sure the pieces sink into the glue or mastic.

In the final grouting process, to secure extruded pieces, build up the grout around those pieces and make sure that all the gaps are filled completely with grout.

Materials

- 8-by-8-by-$3/4$–inch basic wooden picture frame. Precut craft frames and assorted wooden shapes are available at some craft stores, but mostly online.
- Paint color of your choice, if you plan on painting the raw wood
- Vintage baby flowerpot
- Vintage baby bottle and pacifier
- Fifty $3/4$-inch ceramic tiles (black and white)
- Gold and cream-colored china pieces
- Clear glass heart with decoupage image
- Sanded grout (charcoal)
- Mirror or glass insert (if it didn't come with the frame)

59

Tools

- Wheeled glass nipper
- Tile cutter
- Safety glasses
- Paintbrush or foam brush
- Sandpaper
- PVA (Weldbond) adhesive was used for this project, but mastic can also be used
- Roll of painter's tape
- Disposable latex-free gloves
- Large Ziploc bag
- Paper towels
- Q-tips, skewers, toothpicks, or small tools for prodding and cleaning
- Vinegar and water

Directions

1. Cover your workspace with newspaper.
2. If you want to paint the raw wood, do it now and let it dry completely. Keep a little extra paint for any touch-ups that may be needed after grouting.
3. When dry, lightly sand the frame in all of the places where pieces will be glued.
4. With the wheeled glass nipper, cut the baby vase in half. Because I wanted to preserve the "Baby" extrusion from the center of the vase, I started shaping it down to remove it, doing the same with the duck, flowers, and handle on the vase. Reserve the handle, as you can use it someday for a different project.
5. Cut the pink border away from the vase. Cut into similar (smaller) pieces for the inside border.
6. Glue the black and white ceramic tiles around the outer border of the frame, leaving equal space in between each tile for a grout line. Starting with the outer border on this project helps give you a guide to follow while filling in the rest of the frame, with little or no cutting.
7. Attach the baby piece to top center and flower piece to center bottom.
8. Glue the pink border around the mirror opening.
9. Next glue the duck, pacifier, and bottle into place. Fill in gaps by adding the gold hand-cut china pieces.
10. That's it! Let it dry for a minimum of 24 hours.
11. Protect painted areas and delicate objects with painter's tape. Grout the frame. Clean and polish it, then insert a mirror or picture.

White on White

"If you hear a voice within you say, 'You cannot paint,' then by all means paint, and that voice will be silenced." —Vincent van Gogh

There's really nothing better than stumbling across wooden picture frames with wide borders. You can do so much with them. When you want to create a piece with objects protruding from the surface, non-functioning surfaces such as picture frames are one of the best bets for success. Once you've found a place on the wall to hang your piece, the main activity it will see are all of the admirers parading past to view your beautiful work.

The white frame that I used for this project was found on a bottom shelf in the thrift store. If you don't take the effort to really look up, down, and around, you might miss something spectacular! I decided not to paint this one after I fell in love with the worn surface. Instead, I just started gluing.

Wide frames give you an endless array of possibilities. The "White on White" picture frame was created to become a mirror in a ladies dressing area. The little white demitasse cups were the catalyst for the piece and allowed me keep the piece monochromatic (all one color), with a little silver sparkle for old times' sake. I could envision the cups being the perfect place to stash small jewelry or lipsticks in. The little white hanger proved to be the perfect spot to hang necklaces and hair ribbons.

The flat tiles were glued to the frame using a PVA adhesive, and the extruded objects, such as the cups and the wire hanger, were secured using clear Liquid Nails. With the right adhesive, you can glue anything to pretty much anything and get it to stick (within reason, of course). Position it. Glue it.

Check on it. Tape it with painter's tape to secure, and let it dry completely for the best results.

While I sometimes begin a project with a grouping of selected materials, the piece always evolves as I go. It's okay if some of the things that you consider using end up back on the shelf for another time.

This frame reminded me of the large frame I found at a flea market for 25 cents. With it, I created the piece "A Dog's Life," using the dogs that my daughter had collected as a child. She'll get the piece as soon as her kids are old enough to not try to pull the dogs off the frame.

Materials

- Vintage picture frame. Cover or remove picture or mirror, if applicable, before gluing.
- Two white demitasse cups
- Four white china saucers with silver border
- Six strings of white and silver beads
- Fifty 3/4-inch pearly glass sheet tiles
- One hundred pearly micro (3/8- by 3/8-inch, the smallest ceramic tile available) ceramic tiles
- Vintage rhinestone brooch
- Two 1 by 1-inch silver metallic ceramic tiles
- Two acrylic stars
- Hanger
- Sanded grout (white)
- You'll want to purchase a piece of mirror or glass for the frame if it didn't come with one. Local hardware and home improve-ment stores can cut mirror for you at a minimal cost. Check out craft stores to purchase picture glass and backings if you're framing a photo.

Tools

- Wheeled glass nipper
- Tile cutter
- Safety glasses
- Paintbrush or foam brush to paint frame
- Sandpaper
- PVA (Weldbond) adhesive was used for this project, but mastic can also be used
- Roll of painter's tape
- Disposable latex-free gloves
- Large Ziploc bag
- Paper towels
- Q-tips, skewers, toothpicks, or small tools for prodding and cleaning
- Vinegar and water

Directions

1. Cover your workspace with newspaper.
2. If you want to paint the wood, do so now and let it dry com-pletely.
3. Lightly sand the frame in all of the places where pieces will be glued.
4. Cut the border from the plates with the wheeled glass nipper. Make sure the cut pieces lie flat. Keep the size of the pieces similar to each other for visual appeal. Set aside.
5. Glue the pearl micro tiles around the inside border.
6. Take the mesh sheet of pearly glass tiles and cut into strips, preserving the mesh backing.
7. Measure the strips of tile to fit the area to be glued. Glue each strip of pearly glass tiles to the inner borders of the frame.

Look for hangers that can be used for frames at flea markets and yard sales.

8. Secure the demitasse cups with Liquid Nails or mastic, one in each of the bottom corners. Use painter's tape to secure them while drying.

9. Measure string beads and glue the beads on the outer ridge of the frame.

10. Attach the embellished white hanging device with Liquid Nails and secure it with painter's tape until the glue is dry.

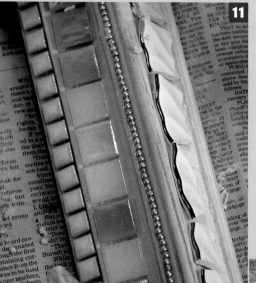

11. Now finish the outside of the frame. Glue the white china border evenly on the outside of the frame, keeping the pieces fairly close together so that you can take advantage of the unique look that a gilded china border will take on after grouting.

12. Attach the brooch and secure with tape.

13. Finish the design by gluing the silver metallic tiles and acrylic hearts into each corner. Secure them with painter's tape.

14. Let the piece dry for a minimum of 24 hours.

15. Tape off delicate pieces, then grout. Clean and polish the frame.

16. Insert a mirror or picture.

Chalk It Up to Fantastic Found Objects

As a dumpster diver and frequent thrift store shopper, I am always on the lookout for cool junk, vessels, frames, mirrors, and pieces of furniture. There really is nothing better than finding a surface that will fill an artistic and functional place in my life. Adding random but functional artwork into my living space distracts from the fact that I can't commit to a wall color other than white. Surprising, I know.

While strolling the aisles at one of my favorite local haunts, I came across this really unique chalkboard and organizer combination. I didn't realize until much later that it wasn't just a chalkboard with storage; it was actually magnetic too. Bonus!

After staring at it for a solid month, inspiration finally hit. Rummaging through my junk shelves, boxes, and basement hideaways, I was able to locate the rest of the dominos that had been my inspiration to dive into the art of mosaic tile some 20 years ago. It's so rare in life to be digging through collections of stuff and piles of junk and actually find what you are looking for. It must have been fate, I guess! It's funny how the dominos ended up being the exact size I needed to border the piece. Things don't always work out so perfectly, so look out for this phenomenon—it's really fun when it sneaks up on you.

Setting the chalkboard on my work table, I started experimenting with other objects to try to come up with a design. I tried buttons, jewelry, tile, polished stones, mirrors, and finally bottle caps. Viola! Bottle caps! It was perfect!

> There's a lot that can be said about the materials you choose for your projects. Sometimes it just takes a little whimsy, luster, and sparkle to bring out the best in a piece.

Moving pieces around on the chalkboard gave me time to think about where this piece would eventually be displayed. A kitchen? Family room? Bar? It occurred to me that since dominos are a game, a game room would be the perfect fit.

Luckily, I had collected some little dishes that resembled dice along the way, and I knew those would work well in this piece. I still needed to figure out exactly where they would make their appearance, but I could figure that out later.

Next, I grabbed some plastic fingers that screw into the wall to act as coat hangers. They were being used in our office, but I just had to have them, so down they came.

And finally, I selected a brown glass tile that would blend with the wood for the inside shelf area, some iridescent glass tile to add interest, and gold mirror tile squares for the outside border.

Materials

- Thrift store chalkboard
- Dominos
- Three little dice-pattern sauce dishes
- Assorted bottle caps
- Two plastic finger coat hangers
- One sheet of glass tile (brown)
- Forty pieces of 3/4-inch pearly iridescent stained glass tile
- One pound of mirrored tiles (gold)
- Sanded grout (charcoal)

Tools

- Safety glasses
- Sandpaper
- PVA (Weldbond) adhesive was used for this project, but mastic can also be used
- Liquid Nails adhesive
- Roll of painter's tape
- Disposable latex-free gloves
- Large Ziploc bag
- Paper towels
- Q-tips, skewers, toothpicks, or small tools for prodding and cleaning
- Vinegar and water

Not a cutting tool in sight

This entire project was completed without a single cut. I didn't plan on that happening, but it did. Lucky me! With dice and dominos all laid out, already in perfect sizes, I should have taken the hint and played the lottery that day.

4. Once the bottle caps are dry, glue the gold mirror tiles to the sides of the piece. There is a method to this madness: if you wait to glue the mirror tiles to the sides last, the piece will be heavier and more fragile than it is right now.

Directions
1. Cover your workspace with newspaper.
2. Lightly sand the wood in all of the places where pieces will be glued.
3. Bottle caps can be somewhat challenging to glue onto things. Mastic is usually a better choice than glue, but you can sink objects into glue, too.

Eyeball the spot where the bottle cap will be placed and apply a circle of glue directly onto the surface. Repeat this process on the back of the bottle cap edge and sink it into the glue. Be prepared to go back and reposition some of the bottle caps that may try to sneak away. Wait for glue to set up a bit before cleaning off any excess.

Be prepared for a piece like this one take multiple days to complete. Mastic will cut down on the slipping of objects and save some time, but you will still have to let certain areas dry before moving on.

When a base is tipped on its side, you have to let it completely dry before flipping it over to tile the other side. Patience is essential. The justification for tiling the sides of an awkward piece early is that fewer tiles will fall off or be damaged this way. Granted, it may take a little more time (a few more days) to complete the project because of drying time, but the problem of pieces falling off will be minimized.

5. Once the sides are completely dry, finish tiling the front of the piece.

6. To balance the outer border with the dominos and finger hooks, play around with them a bit to find the perfect placement before gluing. When you are happy with the way things are laid out, mark a spot and screw the finger hooks into the wood frame. Then glue the dominos into place.

7. Glue the remaining glass tiles to the inside wall and borders of the interior of the piece.

8. Let it dry overnight.

9. Once the chalkboard is completely dry, stand it upright to attach the remaining extruded objects: the dice dishes and Coke glass (which holds the chalk). This is one of those times when you really need to use mastic or an adhesive like Liquid Nails to attach the pieces. When a piece is functional, you want to take extra precautions to make sure the pieces are securely fastened. The good news is that if they do come off, they can always be glued back on.

10

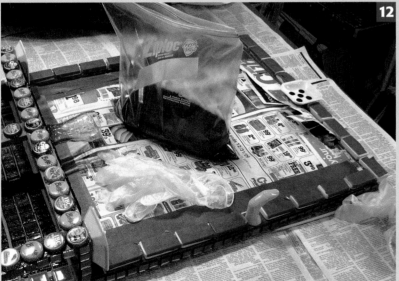

12

10. Embed the dice plates and Coke glass in a "pillow" of adhesive. Try to watch the amount of adhesive being used. You really don't want to have tons of glue or mastic seeping out from underneath set objects. If you do have excess adhesive peeking out, let it set up for just a bit and carefully clean off the excess using a wooden skewer and paper towel. Afterward, reposition objects if necessary.

11. Let your masterpiece dry for a minimum of 24 hours. Make sure everything is secure.

12. Tape the back of the piece and any delicate surfaces with painter's tape before grouting.

13. Grout the project.

Regrouting

Wet grout doesn't like to attach itself to grout that has already dried. If something falls off after you have grouted the piece and there are remnants of grout or adhesives in its place, grab a Dremel tool and clean the area thoroughly before reattaching objects with glue. Let it dry. Try to carefully regrout the cleaned area. You never know; sometimes it works.

The finished piece, ready for display!

Bowl You Over

Finding discarded bowls is a joy in and of itself. Some of these vessels once functioned in some important capacity when they were with their original owners, while others were merely decorative.

Creating mosaic tile bowls is one of the best ways to help you perfect your skill at hand-cutting china. Remember that whenever you are tiling a surface that is rounded and/or functioning in some way, you have to be aware of sharp edges and pieces that don't lie flat on the surface. The smaller the piece of china, the flatter it will lie. You will get there with practice, patience, and perseverance.

Place settings of china (preferably different sizes of the same pattern) are the perfect inspiration for mosaic tile bowls. If you choose a single pattern of china, you will have a consistent thickness of working materials to

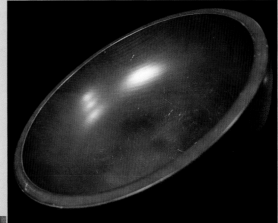

help keep things flat. Older china pieces are, generally speaking, made from more delicate materials and easier to cut. Look for place settings with full patterns, great borders, and centers that can be cut out.

After a bowl is tiled, it can be used in limited functions. I really don't recommend serving food in it. It's also very important to note that tiled bowls weigh quite a bit more once they are grouted. Keep the weight in mind when finding a spot to display your piece, especially if you have small children.

You can choose to tile the entire bowl, or just the inside. Just remember, if you tile the bottom of the bowl, you will want to make sure that it doesn't wobble from uneven pieces or scratch the finish of the surface you display it on.

I have glued flat square gems and marbles onto the bottom of bowls for feet and had great success. If you do this, set the bowl on the gems to try them out before you glue them on.

Materials
- Wooden bowl
- One place setting or multiple pieces of one china pattern
- Mirrored tile—about 1/2 pound
- Iridescent stained glass tiles (complementary colors)
- Sanded grout in complementary color

Bowl projects can take a couple days to complete. Mastic will cut down on the slipping of objects and save some time, but you will still have to let certain areas dry completely before moving on.

Tools

- Wheeled glass nippers
- Safety glasses
- Sandpaper
- PVA (Weldbond) adhesive was used for this project, but mastic can also be used
- Weighted coffee can—helpful to rest the bowl on when tiling the back
- A revolving server or lazy susan can be used to help rotate the bowl for gluing without continual handling
- Roll of painter's tape
- Disposable latex-free gloves
- Large Ziploc bag
- Paper towels
- Q-tips, skewers, toothpicks, or small tools for prodding and cleaning
- Vinegar and water

Directions

1. Cover your workspace with newspaper.
2. Hand-cut a substantial quantity of china pieces and tiles. Set aside. Preserve what you can: plate edges, centers, and backs.
3. Lightly sand the bowl to roughen the surface.
4. Cut mirror tiles in half and glue them onto the top rim of the bowl.
5. Being careful not to disrupt the mirror tiles, carefully start to fill the inside of the bowl with hand-cut flat china pieces. Stop halfway up to make sure that you leave enough room around the top of the bowl to attach china or tile border pieces. Stop at this point and let the glue dry. Come back to it when the pieces seem fairly secure.

6. Shape the border pieces that you cut from the plates into a fairly uniform size to give your bowl a smooth, finished edge.

7. Tip the bowl on one side, brace it against something secure, and start to glue the border pieces to the inside rim of the bowl, beginning with the side facing you. When you are gluing pieces in this area, keep them even with the mirror tiles that are already glued to the top rim. With the bowl still on its side, continue gluing. If the pieces start slipping, take a break and let it dry for a bit.

8. Check back in about a half hour or so and rotate the bowl to finish gluing the remaining section.

9. If you've left enough room to lay a row of a complementary-colored tile, repeat the gluing process, letting each section dry before moving on to the next.

10. Fill in any remaining open space with more of the hand-cut china pieces. Let the piece dry for at least 24 hours before tiling the back.

11. Tiling the back of a bowl is very similar to tiling the inside of a bowl. Since it's curved, pieces need to lie flat. If tiles are slipping, divide the gluing process into about four manageable sections. Prop the bowl up on something secure and wait for each section to dry before moving on to the next.

12. Once the piece is completely tiled, let it dry for a minimum of 24 hours.

13. Grout the bowl. If you have decided not to tile the entire bowl, don't forget to protect the exposed wood with painter's tape before grouting.

Wooden Objects

"To live a creative life, we must lose our fear of being wrong."
—Joseph Chilton Pierce

Pre-cut wooden shapes and discarded wooden surfaces make great bases for mosaics. Whether the wood pieces are finished or unfinished, the versatility allows you to be extremely creative in the design process. The finished projects are simple but very artistic!

Living in the Midwest has taught me an important lesson about gluing bits and pieces onto wooden bases: you never know if they can survive the elements. When in doubt, don't use wood. But if you must, bring mosaic tile projects that have been created on wood inside during the colder months. Brush on a coat of grout sealer before putting the project back outside in the warmer months.

The simple wood mittens and shoes that I used in this chapter were picked up at a flea market. Just adding a few materials to unique wooden shapes will give you all of the inspiration you'll need to create another, and another, and another.

Materials
- Wood shapes
- Mirrored tiles, broken ornament pieces, and stained glass
- Assorted glass hearts
- Paint color of your choice, if you plan on painting the wood. I did not paint the surfaces for this project, although I did sand the wood before gluing.
- Sanded grout (charcoal)

Tools
- Wheeled glass nipper
- Safety glasses
- Paint or foam brush
- Sandpaper
- PVA (Weldbond) adhesive was used for this project, but mastic can also be used
- Disposable latex-free gloves
- Large Ziploc bag
- Paper towels
- Q-tips, skewers, toothpicks, or small tools for prodding and cleaning
- Vinegar and water

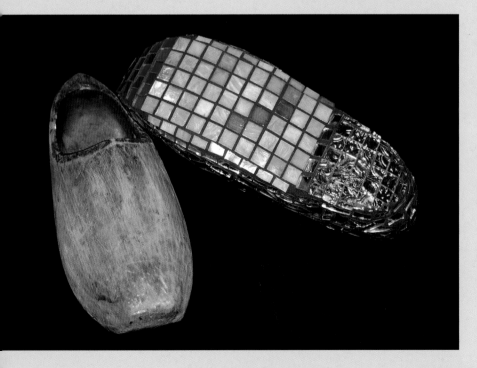

Directions

1. Cover your workspace with newspaper.
2. Lightly sand the wood to roughen the surface.
3. Cut the mirrors and tiles into workable pieces with wheeled glass nipper. Set them aside.
4. Brush a coat of Weldbond or another PVA adhesive onto to the surface. Let dry.
5. Start gluing the pieces on. You can do this randomly, or in a preplanned pattern. Glue the pieces fairly close together for a grout line that will enhance, not take over. Clean off the excess glue as you go.

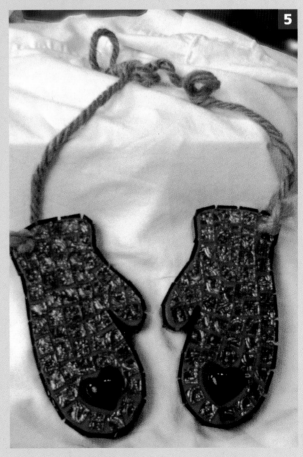

6. Let each side dry before flipping the piece over.
7. Wait a minimum of 24 hours
   before grouting.
8. Grout and clean.

Something in the Air

You could say that I have a fascination with certain found objects. In particular, I seem to find myself collecting a lot of old metal and wooden fireplace match holders. Perhaps it's because these little treasures not only hold long matches, but incense as well.

In any case, they're always a great conversation starter for all who enter my home!

This is a fun and easy project to create. A favorite of mine, this project allows me to whip up unique gifts for the special people in my life. I hope they enjoy receiving them as much as I enjoy making them!

The great thing about the size of this project is that it only takes a couple of hours. A few odds and ends, a little glue, a box of fireplace matches (or incense), a bit of gift wrap, and a bow, and violà! You have a charming gift.

Materials

- Wood or metal fireplace match holder
- Assorted mirror, glass, and ceramic tiles
- Old jewelry
- Marbles and gems
- Glass hearts
- Random game pieces
- Charms
- Milliefori
- Miniature picture frames can be filled with images and then glued to the surface. Take time to cover the frames with painter's tape to protect them before grouting.
- Sanded grout in preferred color. Dark grout is most common, but if you create thinner grout lines you can expect better results with lighter grout colors.

Tools

- Wheeled glass nipper
- Tile cutter
- Safety glasses
- Paintbrush or foam brush
- Sandpaper
- PVA (Weldbond) adhesive was used for this project, but mastic can also be used
- Roll of painter's tape
- Disposable latex-free gloves
- Large Ziploc bag
- Paper towels
- Q-tips, skewers, toothpicks, or small tools for prodding and cleaning
- Vinegar and water

Directions

1. Cover your workspace with newspaper.
2. Lightly sand the wood or coat the metal with PVA glue to prepare the surface.
3. Play with various materials to come up with a design.
4. Cut pieces of similar size to create simple patterns. Set aside.
5. Start gluing the pieces onto the front of the holder. Fill the remaining areas to complete while the piece is still lying flat. Let dry.

6. Turning the piece onto its side, glue on mirror squares. Let the glue set up for a bit so that the pieces don't fall off when you flip the piece to glue the other side. Why fight it? Waiting for things to dry actually saves time!
7. Turn to piece over to the other side and glue on the tesserae. Let dry on its side.
8. Let the completed piece dry a minimum of 24 hours before grouting.
9. Cover delicate materials with painter's tape, then grout. Clean the incense holder and let it dry.

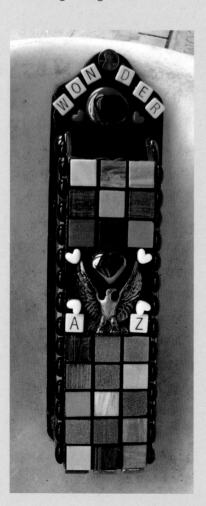

Add-ons

Pair the match/incense holder with a block of wood (at least 10 by 4 by 3/4-inch) that has been covered with complementary china or tile and an incense ring to round out the set.

Set in Stone

"So you see, imagination needs moodling—long, inefficient, happy idling, dawdling and puttering." —Brenda Ueland

Gluing shards to concrete surfaces, statuary, and birdbaths is not much different from tiling a wooden surface. The biggest difference is the preparation, adhesive choice, and upkeep.

When gluing directly onto concrete there are a couple of things that you must do to assure your success.

Preparing Concrete Before Gluing

Tools and materials

- Box of trisodium phosphate (TSP)
- Concrete patch, if repairs are needed. This can be found in most home improvement stores.
- Concrete sealer
- Rubber gloves
- Bucket
- Wire brush
- Foam paint brushes
- Rags
- Drop cloth or layers of newspaper

Directions

1. Mix the trisodium phosphate in a bucket according to the directions. TSP is a popular cleaner that helps ensure that the surface is free of dirt, grime, or grease. Objects glued to a clean concrete surface will have a much stronger hold.
2. Scrub the piece with a wire brush.
3. Let dry completely.
4. If you see cracks in the concrete that need to be repaired, fix them now with a concrete patch. Let dry.
5. Seal the concrete according to the instructions on the package of concrete sealer. Let dry.

Adhesives

Working with concrete means that you have to have the proper adhesives to assure that your finished project will withstand the outdoor elements—especially if you live in a colder or rainy climate. Use a thinset mortar or waterproof silicone adhesive.

Thinset mortar is made from a combination of cement, aggregates, and special additives designed for attaching rock, stone, tile, china, and porcelain to concrete surfaces. You can purchase it pre-mixed or in a powdered form that you mix yourself. The benefit of thinset mortar, besides its strength, is that it gives you a fair amount of working time to move the pieces around. Thinset won't solidify for at least 2 to 4 hours (but it takes at least 24 hours to dry); however, I would still suggest working in small sections to prevent it from drying out.

Since thinset mortar has a tendency to crack, you need to find one that is polymer or latex modified. Thinset is usually white or gray.

I purchase thinset mortar at my local home improvement and tile store, under several different brand names. I've been happy enough with those choices to stop looking for a better alternative.

For small projects, butter the mortar onto the back of the piece with a popsicle stick and glue the pieces onto the base. For larger projects, use a trowel or other spreading tool to spread the thinset directly onto the surface and push the pieces directly into the mortar. Remember to clean off any excess mortar before grouting.

The concrete mushrooms shown in this chapter were cleaned with TSP and allowed to dry. Concrete sealer was then applied.

Pieces were buttered with a silicone adhesive and applied to the mushrooms and then left to dry for 24 hours.

Sanded grout was used, but instead of mixing the grout with water, I used a liquid latex additive to make the grout more flexible and help to ward off future cracking.

Once the piece was grouted, cleaned and dry, I sealed it with grout sealer. As always, read the directions when using this kind of product.

Try to keep the piece free from dirt by applying a coat of grout sealer at least once a year.

One of a Kind

"Creativity is inventing, experimenting, growing, taking risks, breaking rules, making mistakes, and having fun." —Mary Lou Cook

The accumulation of things to glue on is never-ending. Until recently, I have had a difficult time throwing anything away. Well, truth be told, I still do. Treasured finds magically appear, and I just have to have them to cover with shards of another time and place.

The ongoing opportunities that present you with perfect tables, dressers, headboards, pedestals, and unique surfaces that need to be decorated are overwhelming. How do you walk away from a piece that brings you a creative boost and artistic enthusiasm?

It can be challenging in the beginning stages of this art form. You may find yourself becoming a pack rat, and defending your treasures like a junkyard dog with the justification that this is the stuff that you'll get around to gluing one day.

You may get around to some; some you most assuredly won't. In the meantime, the art of found objects can take over your basement, closets, garage, and kitchen. Try to establish a few boundaries, for the sanity of yourself and your loved ones.

I'll give you fair warning: it's a challenge to keep this very random art form organized!

Pique assiette furniture
When you are creating pique assi-ette mosaic tile furniture, all of the standard preparations, tools, materials, and directions apply, along with additional safety precautions.

Always make sure that the piece you have chosen to tile has the ability to withstand the additional weight associated with this art form. When selecting a piece of furniture, check to make sure that it is a stable piece of wooden or metal furniture (I don't recommend tiling on plastic). If the piece is unstable or needs to be repaired, fix it before you begin to make sure that the piece is safe and suitable to use.

As with all functioning mosaic tile artwork, check that the tiles and shards that are glued to the surface are free from sharp edges.

The "Finger Cutter" was one of my very early furniture pieces. It's a perfect example of what not to do. Some of the shards are sharp and oversized, based on where they were glued. It has proven to be a dangerous piece to move if you grab it wrong. It's not something I like to worry about, especially with grandchildren running around.

Sure, it's a cool piece. I love it! I just don't want it out in the open until I can get around to smoothing out the edges.

Mosaic tile furniture tips and tricks

■ Frame the edges of tables, chairs, dressers, and pedestals with smooth-edged tile or glass to allow people to actually use the piece without it cutting them or snagging their clothes.

Pack Rat Advice

Select the surface and materials that you have decided on. Make that project your only concern. If you start it, finish it, and find a place for it.

You may decide to have two projects going on at the same time. That's fine. But if the bits and pieces start to take over your living space, there may not be any room left for creativity.

- Keep the thickness of materials consistent on tabletops. You don't want glasses or plates to wobble or tip over when placed on the finished surface.
- Clean and sand the surface before beginning.
- PVA adhesive, clear silicone, and mastic can all be used on furniture.
- When tiling larger pieces of furniture, divide the gluing process into sections.
- Set aside multiple hours to create the piece. Allow drying time in between sections. Add more time if you've decided to add tile around legs of tables or chairs.
- Work with small pieces that will lie flat. Patience is a must. That's the best advice I can give.

Make sure the seat doesn't have sharp edges.

The "Anchors Aweigh" bedside table shows how a napkin holder, a pelican souvenir, a coaster, a little box, and lots of glass tile can bring a number of functions to a very small table in a really unique way.

- Think of ways to embed unique objects that offer a function to the piece. After deciding where the finished piece will be displayed, devise ways to incorporate items that will serve a purpose—a pen holder, key dish, or a coin catch-all. The sky's the limit! Glue extruded pieces with additional adhesive—preferably clear Liquid Nails or mastic. After the adhesive has set up a bit, remove the excess. Build up extra grout around these objects.

- Use a latex additive instead of water, when mixing grout for a furniture piece.

- Keep the surface free of spills, dirt, and grease.

- Seal the grout at least once a year if the piece is used often.

- If pieces fall off of the furniture due to wear and tear, use a Dremel tool to clean out the remaining adhesive or grout from the area. Re-glue the pieces. Let dry, grout carefully, and hope for the best.

A tiled dog house that I'm sure Buster would love!

Glass Objects

"You use a glass mirror to see your face; you use works of art to see your soul." —George Bernard Shaw

For many years I rarely, if ever, found myself venturing into the world of glass. All I can ask myself now is "why?"

It was fear of cutting, I suppose. I can barely cut a straight line with a scissors, let alone a glass-cutter. But one day I found an abandoned bucket of stained glass pieces on my doorstep. "Okay, I see you," I said. "Now what am I suppose to do with you?"

Being completely aware of my limitations, I was surprised to find that cutting glass isn't as difficult as you might think. Taking a couple of classes taught me the basic fundamentals of cutting stained glass, and I have been perfecting my skills ever since.

Unlike true stained glass artists, found object artists aren't as concerned about the type of glass we're incorporating into a piece. If we like the sparkle and can cut it, we'll glue it.

Stained glass comes in an endless supply of colors and textures, in precut sheets, squares, and irregular pieces. You can also use some of the oodles of clear and colored glass objects and dishes available to found object artists. With thousands of colors, shapes, and sizes to choose from, glass provides an overwhelming treasure trove of unique brilliance. I highly recommend adding beautiful glass into your material mix; it adds a depth to a piece that you will be hard pressed to find with other materials.

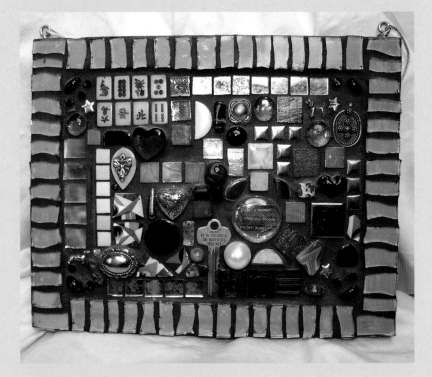

Working With Glass

Key things to remember when working with glass objects

■ Do not glue objects to glass surfaces that don't have a solid frame or aren't sturdy. If you think the frame, glass, or both might not be able to hold the weight of your completed piece, find a different surface. Larger pieces can get very heavy and can be a real hazard (and huge mess) if they fall from the wall or window.

- Gluing to glass takes preparation and patience.
- Always wear safety glasses.
- Have a first aid kit handy, just in case.
- Make sure the surfaces and glass pieces are clean and dry before gluing.

Cutting glass dishware

This is one of those cutting techniques where you should err on the side of caution. You never know how a piece of glass will react to you taking a small hammer or a wheeled glass nipper to it. ALWAYS, and I mean always, wear your safety glasses and put the glass object underneath a thick towel to keep the shards under control. First, tap the piece firmly, but not too hard, with a small hammer. This helps break up the glass into more manageable sections. After the pieces are broken down, you can attempt to carefully cut the glass into even smaller pieces with a wheeled glass nipper.

Caution: Glass is sharp and very unpredictable. Always wear safety glasses before cutting glass of any kind.

Cutting stained glass sheets into strips

I've had the greatest success cutting stained glass using an oiled glass cutter, running pliers, and a cork-backed ruler. Line up your ruler. Mark the line, if needed.

Start the cutter about 1/4 inch from the end of the glass. Keep your forearm straight. Push down gently but firmly and slide the cutter straight along the ruler, making only one pass. Line up the score on the glass with the line on a pair of running pliers. Snap it. If you did it right, it should come off in a perfect strip. If not, simply try

again. Squares can be cut from the stained glass strip using the wheeled glass nippers. If the squares aren't coming out with a mostly straight edge, the wheels on the nippers may need to be replaced. Or you can score the glass again with the oiled glass cutter and repeat the process with the running pliers.

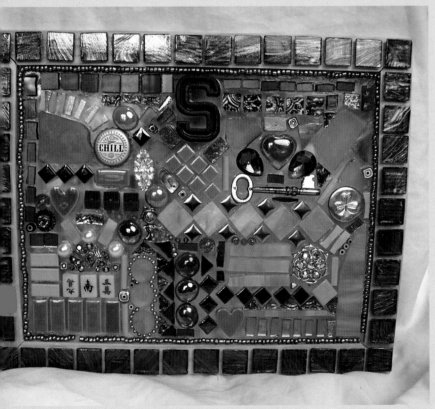

Glass on Glass

Glass on glass is a technique that allows you to create a funky glass window or wall hanging using unique glass, plates, tiles, china, glass gems, mirrors, stained glass, game pieces, and other random materials.

Using a simple wood frame with a sturdy glass insert is the easiest way to get your feet wet with this unique mosaic style. It's very easy to find cheap wooden frames with a 1/2-to-1–inch border that are perfect for this project. Many of the cheaper frames come with very thin glass or plexiglass, so you'll have to take the frame to a local home improvement store or hardware store and have them cut you a thicker piece of glass to fit the frame. Using Weldbond adhesive, glue the glass into the frame and let it dry overnight.

Once the glass is ready, gather your materials and start designing the piece. When you're comfortable with the design, begin gluing the pieces directly onto the glass with Weldbond adhesive. Clean up excess adhesive as you're working. The completed piece can be grouted or left as it is.

The Kitchen Window

While driving down the California coast, I stopped to explore the little seaside village of Cambria. There in the display of an antique store was an old window frame that had been embellished with butter dishes, glass plates, stained glass chunks, gems, and random pieces of unique glass patterns. It was stunning! It was beyond my budget, so I took a photo.

Arriving home, I wanted to recreate that piece and knew that I would have to test a few adhesives to see which ones would be best for the job.

"Six Panes" (at right) was created using Weldbond, as a test. I was semi-successful with my efforts: some of the adhesive didn't dry clear due to the lack of air under the pressed glass pieces. The affected pieces had be removed, cleaned, and reapplied. Luckily, Weldbond is more forgiving than other adhesives, so with a little

patience, safety glasses, and a few tools, I pried the pieces off without breaking the window. This allowed me to reapply the bad pieces using GE Silicone II. Keep in mind that if you are using a silicone adhesive or clear Liquid Nails, you will not be able to remove the pieces once the adhesive is dry.

"Everything but the Kitchen Sink" (below) was created using clear Liquid Nails. It proved easier to apply the adhesive directly onto the glass pieces and gently press them onto the window. Be cautious about the amount of glue you are using. Try not to move the glued pieces around

very much to keep glue trails to a minimum. Make sure to try and clean any excess adhesive from around the pieces after it has set up a bit. Since the piece wasn't going to be grouted, I tried to set the pieces very close together to provide more privacy as a window covering.

Glass on glass projects are always favorites in the classes I teach.

Glass Collage

Glass collage, or "crash glass," has hit the found object world by storm! This unique art form uses collected imagery, exotic papers, and photos, hiding them under shattered windshield and tempered glass. Papers and such are glued to the surface with an epoxy adhesive. Then pieces of shattered tempered glass and broken windshield glass (crash glass) are glued on top of the imagery, allowed to dry, and grouted. The results are extraordinary! Mo Ringey and Ellen Blakely are two artists who brought the amazing crash glass art form to life. You can check out their work on their wonderful websites, www.ellenblakeley.com and www.moringey.com.

Being a collage artist first, I couldn't wait to learn how to blend two of my very favorite pastimes, decoupage and mosaic tile. Taking a "crash glass" class with Laurel Skye got me thinking. I've been gluing images behind glass for years, and I've been pretty successful achieving very similar results using a more simplified, less messy process. A wooden trivet makes a great "crash glass" project for beginners!

Materials
- Wooden trivet
- Shattered tempered glass
- Interesting papers (don't use inkjet copies or newspaper—it will smear)
- Foam paint brush
- Paint color of choice
- Weldbond

Tools
- Safety glasses
- Wheeled glass cutter
- Hammer
- Heavier kitchen towel

Directions

- Paint your surface. Let dry.
- Arrange glass and images on the surface.
- Cut glass to match up with your selected images,
- Arrange the design onto the surface.
- Once you're satisfied with the design, use a foam brush to apply a smooth layer of Weld-bond onto the back of each piece of glass that will have imagery behind it. Don't get carried away with the glue. Just brush on enough to attach the picture to the glass.
- Carefully apply the images so that they show through the glass. Gently smooth.
- Let the glue dry completely, then glue the pieces of glass to the surface of your piece. Adding a little more drying time will allow the adhesive to turn from white to clear.

Instead of gluing the images to the glass, I chose to de-coupage background layers of selected papers directly to the surface of my trivet to cover the entire area. Covering the surface with images gives it a more uniform and interesting look, with no black holes.

- Continue to glue images and glass around the piece.
- Let dry overnight.
- Grout.

Rock on Glass

Dave Beckius—
The Agate Man
www.polishedagatemosaics.com

Dave and I met when he came in to register his wife and himself for an upcoming mosaic tile class. Not realizing how much the classes were, he was cheerfully pulling out his wallet as I said, "That will be a hundred ninety dollars."

All the blood left his face, but he had already made up his mind, so he handed me his credit card.

The night of the class, Dave walked in with a bucket of polished rocks. He appeared to still be a little put off by the cost of the class—at least, that was my perception. As he sat down, he set the bucket of rocks on the table and said, "What can I do with these?" It was as though he were challenging me to come up with a completely new mosaic tile project that blended with his hobby of rock collecting.

Well, it wasn't the class that the other four people attending paid for, but I'm always up for a challenge! Luckily, I had already glued a new piece of glass into a simple wooden frame days before. Laying the frame in front of him, along with a bottle of Weldbond and some vitreous glass tiles for the border, I responded with, "Here you go, start gluing."

That's all it took.

Now, Dave's rock tumblers run 24/7, polishing thousands of extraordinary stones and slicing them to the perfect size to create breathtaking polished agate mosaics.

With his pieces flying off his garage shelves, he has earned a place in a variety of juried art shows and finds that he is now rubbing elbows with rock aficionados around the world.

Frequently Asked Questions

"All great deeds and all great thoughts have a ridiculous beginning."
—Albert Camus

How much tile or china do I need for my project?

The lists of materials offered here will give you a general idea of how much tile or china you will need for the projects in this book. As a general rule of thumb, 225 3/4-inch tiles will cover one square foot. If you're using different sized tiles, china pieces, and shards in your projects, you may have to eyeball it, but if you want to get a more accurate materials count, you can locate free mosaic tile calculators online.

How can I create a mosaic tile address plaque?

I'd suggest creating the piece on concrete backer board that has been prepared with holes to use to attach it to the house. Use a waterproof/weatherproof thinset as the adhesive, and trace the address onto the board using stencils. Mix the grout with a latex additive, and seal the grout once it has dried.

How do I tile a backsplash?

Working on vertical services can be a challenge. If you're creating a backsplash with complementary tile that is already glued onto mesh sheets, it's a breeze.

But if you have random pieces of all shapes and sizes, it takes a little bit of preparation and patience. First, score the wall surface to roughen it a bit. Then you can go right at it with a notched trowel and mastic. Apply mastic to a manageable area, push pieces into the mastic, and wait for them to grab hold. If you have pieces that extrude, like cups and such, they will have to be glued to the wall and then secured with small nails to help hold them in place while the mastic dries. When the adhesive is dry, remove the nails before grouting.

Materials
- Tile mesh
- Concrete backer board cut to size
- Drill and appropriate screws to attach the board to the wall
- Notched trowel
- Thinset or mastic
- Tile cutter

- Wheeled glass nippers
- Tape measure
- Tiles and random objects
- Tile spacers, if applicable
- Rubber gloves
- Bucket or pail
- Rubber grout float
- Grout and latex grout additive instead of water
- Grout sealer (functioning mosaic tile projects should always be sealed)
- Sponge (look for one with small holes)
- Vinegar and water

Easy backsplash installation
1. Measure the backsplash area and divide it into equal, workable sections.
2. Cut a piece of tile mesh for each section.
3. Glue the mesh to measured and equally sized concrete backer board.
4. Drill holes in the board now, so that the piece can be screwed onto the wall along with a layer of adhesive for a secure hold.
5. Lay out the backsplash design idea on the mesh before gluing.
6. Glue the objects to the meshed board. Let dry for 24 hours or more.

7. Score the wall to roughen the surface.
8. Take one section at a time. Apply mastic to the wall using the notched trowel. Push a section of tiled board into the mastic. Make sure the screw holes are free of adhesive.
9. Let the panel dry, then screw it into place. Repeat with all sections. At this point, I'd let the mastic set up and dry before grouting.
10. Once the mastic is dry, grout.

You could grout each section on a flat surface before installing it, but you will have a noticeable gap between each of the sections that won't be grouted. Besides, the weight of each section is more difficult to manage if it's already grouted. Unfortunately, it's almost impossible to get grout to stick to itself after it's dried. It's really a lot easier to make sure to blend all of the sections by applying the grout directly to the wall.

How do I make a stepping stone?

1. Find a form. You can use a ready-made form or something found around the house that could be suitable for a stepping stone.
2. Purchase the concrete of your choice. There are many. Quick setting concrete is not recommended, for obvious reasons. Ask questions at the home improvement store to determine which concrete is most suitable.
3. Gather materials to decorate the stepping stone.
4. Mix the concrete according to the directions. If you live in a cold climate, make sure to take temperature into consideration when choosing the concrete.
5. Spray form with a cooking oil spray, such as PAM.
6. Pour concrete into form.
7. Push materials into concrete before it dries.
8. Let the stepping stone dry for at least 3 days.
9. Pop it out, seal it, and plant it.

How do I tile a patio table?

Make sure the table will support the weight before you even attempt to apply tile or shards to it. Don't tile directly onto the glass that the patio table came with. Instead, have a piece of concrete backer board cut to fit the table. Secure and reinforce. Score the surface. Apply materials using mastic or thinset. Let it dry, grout, and seal. If you live in a cold climate, it's best to store the table inside during colder months.

What is the best adhesive?

Consider the surface you're using, the location where the piece will rest, and whether the piece is used on a daily basis. These answers will influence the type of adhesive you will choose. There's literally an adhesive for every situation. The best way is to start by reading the application section on any and all adhesives before you buy. Ask questions! What you don't know will affect the outcome.

The jury is still out in the mosaic tile world when it comes to the best adhesives. I believe you have to try a few to see what works best for you. My favorites are listed in the adhesives section of the book. Unless someone comes up with something spectacular, these are the products I stick with.

Tip

Wear old clothes when tiling walls. Use drop cloths to protect floors, counters, and appliances before grouting.

A Brief History of Found Object Art

"I like it because it tells so much about my story . . . life smashes things to bits and you glue it back together to make something beautiful with the pieces." —an unknown mosaic artist

The Victorian era is sometimes regarded as a creative dry period in the timeline of modern civilization because of its reputation for moral austerity and the widespread emphasis on the virtues of dignity and restraint. But in spite of—or because of—this social climate, many types of art actually flourished. Shard art, a type of mosaic tile technique, was one of those mediums. It was popularized by Victorian men and women who began turning their broken pieces of china, old jewelry, and glass into new decorative objects such as vases, flower pots, and tables. These new creations were also called "putty pots," a name derived from the putty used to affix the found objects to the vessels and surfaces, and "memory ware," in reference to the sentimental value of the materials.

The contemporary name of "pique assiette" came into being in 1938 when Raymond Edouard Isidore, an average Joe from Chartres, began gluing stuff to other stuff, namely found objects, pieces of broken glass, and remnants of pottery to his home and gardens near Paris. The townspeople gave him the nickname Picassiette, which means "stealer from plates"—a moocher or a freeloader. Can't you just imagine the exchanges of the locals?

"I saw Picassiette down at le café last week. Mon dieu! I could have sworn I caught sight of him concealing his dinner plate down his trousers!"

"Sacré bleu! That monsieur certainly risks his derrière for the sake of his ridiculous object d'art."

"Oui."

Today, Raymond Edouard Isidore is regarded as a visionary. His home, now known as La Maison Picassiette, is treasured as a work of art—the extraordinary result of this man's work, accomplished over a span of 26 years. Visitors from all over the world derive inspiration from the house and garden he covered with intricate mosaics. Although scholars and admirers alike have tried to pinpoint the source of this everyday laborer's revelation, or discover the identity of his muse, I believe that the truth is plain to see: his natural creativity simply met its ideal form of expression. Throughout history, this has been the catalyst for life-changing, world-changing art.

We are, after all, still talking about him. The nickname Picassiette stuck (no pun intended) in a big way. As if part of a giant, 75-year-old game of Telephone, the word slowly evolved into pique assiette, the contemporary name for shard art, Today, you can view public and historical examples of pique assiette all around the world. I guess you could call these found object artists the pioneers of the recycled art movement.

Popular and Famous Mosaic Tile Destinations

La Maison Picassiette
Raymond Isidore
Chartres, France

Raymond Isidore's devotion to the project left behind a family home and garden covered in intricate mosaics made of tiles, crockery, and magical found objects

The Rock Garden
Nek Chand Saini
Chandigarh, India

The Rock Garden, now acknowledged as one of the modern wonders of the world, is said to be the greatest artistic achievement seen in India since the Taj Mahal.

The Tarot Garden
Niki De Saint Phalle
Capalbio, Italy

Influenced by Parque Güell, Niki de Saint Phalle decided that she wanted to create a garden of whimsical sculptures inspired by the symbols found on Tarot cards. After more than twenty years of work, the garden, called Giardino dei Tarocchi in Italian, was completed in 1998.

Watts Towers
Simon Rodia
Los Angeles, California

Simon Rodia (above) spent thirty-four years in the early 1900s building the seventeen Watts Towers and decorating them with mosaics of tile, broken glass, seashells, and other found objects.

Mosaic Trail
Jim Powers
New York City

Jim Powers created the mosaic trail on a series of light poles (approximaterly eighty light poles total) across New York City's Lower East Side and Greenwich Village. Made of broken dishes and tiles, the mosaic trail took five years to complete.

Parque Güell
Antonio Gaudi
Barcelona, Spain

Parque Guell is the amazing work of Antonio Gaudi. built in the years 1900 to 1914. Gaudi designed and created the tile garden to bring the peace and calm that one would expect from a walk in the park.

You can visit many of the mosaic tile wonders of the world online:

- Joy of Shards:
  www.thejoyofshards.co.uk
- Mosaic Matters:
  www.mosaicmatters.co.uk
- Mosaic Atlas:
  www.mosaicatlas.com

Other fun mosaic tile place to visit:
- Weird Gardens:
  www.weirdgardens.com
- The House of Shards:
  www.ucmmuseum.com/
  shards.htm

Resources

Mosaic Tile Organizations

Society of American Mosaic
    Artists (SAMA)
    www.americanmosaics.org
British Association for Modern
    Mosaic (BAMM)
    www.bamm.org.uk

Mosaic Tile Tools and Materials

- 225 Water Street Creative Arts
    www.225waterstreet.com
- Hakatai
    www.hakatai.com
- Diamond Tech
    www.diamondtechglass.com
- Mosaic Smalti
    www.mosaicsmalti.com
- Delphi Glass
    www.delphiglass.com
- Murano Millehori
    www.muranomillefiori.com
- Mosaic Mercantile
    www.mosaicmercantile.com

Adhesives
- Weldbond Adhesive
    www.weldbondusa.com
- Douglas & Sturgess (epoxy)
    douglasandsturgess.com

Acknowledgments

Pausing to consider and recognize all inspiration through time, tribulation, and triumph, and startled to find myself in a position to honor those influences, I knew this would be a tome of indebtedness. From those that encouraged and gave me belief to those that dismissed my art, inversely blessing me with determination, I must apologize for not saluting you all individually, as my publisher has promised to play me off the stage in an Oscar-type manner before the end of the book. But you know who you are and I know you're out there. I can hear you reading. Thank you. Thank you.

Then there are those who I must pay printed homage to, out of a pure appreciation for allowing my creativity to escape, and those who I will continue to be dependant on for birthday gifts and holiday cards.

To my soulmate, and best friend, Rob. Your love, creative vision, gentle support, laughter, and wisdom will always give me just what I need, at just the right time. It's really true . . . you do make things magically appear. *Isn't this fun!*

My beautiful children, Carly and David . . . while there is no way to express what it meant to me, bringing the two of you into this experience, you both know how very much I love you. I wanted to thank you for the joy and amazement that you have always brought into my life. It was really fun growing up with you. *Are we there yet?*

Special thanks to my mom Beetsie for always going crazy over my artwork.

Miss Alice, words can't describe what a blessing it is to have you call me your friend.

Arcata or Bust!

My lovely friend Mindy, thank you for always being the one really true friend and the other half of the "Dumpster Diving Diva Duo."

My heartfelt thanks to Jenna Eileen Barsness, for her enthusiasm, information, suggestions, and *wry* humor in the editing of this project.

To my girl Karen, for riding the colorfully wild side of life with me. *Arms up, everybody!*

And finally, to the little blessings in my life . . . kisses to Tyler, Jason, Raquelle, Luke, Tyler, and Jacob . . . for their creative, funny, pure unbridled imagination that will continue timelessly to be the very core my own discovery and the ability to live it each and every day.

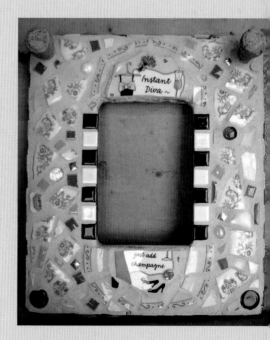

My Artist's Journey

My weekly stop to the craft store was always a wonderful, but lengthy, experience. My mind would race as I tried to decide which art or craft project to conquer next. I knitted, crocheted, sewed, stamped, beaded, wrapped wire, painted, threw clay, and tried my hand at making jewelry. Like most normal, well-adjusted human beings, I completed some craft projects with gusto and others, well . . . not so much. While a fraction of us are lucky enough to find our true artistic passion without much of a search, others have a room full of unfinished craft projects awaiting our return (not that there's anything wrong with that!). It really doesn't matter, as long as we continue to create.

Concentrating on one art form was a challenge for me until I discovered pique assiette. More than two decades ago, I purchased a vintage card table and chairs from an estate sale. The leather inlay on the tabletop was worn, and the chair cushions were brittle from age. I knew that someday I'd get around to refurbishing that piece with a beautiful photo collage and paint. I carried that set around with me for years (well, not literally), as I could never bring myself to part with it. I felt that it had a purpose beyond taking up space in my hatchback. Of course, no one ever sat at this table. From time to time, I would look at it with remorse, imagining the voice of Marlon Brando chiding me, "You shoulda looked out for it a little bit. It coulda had class! It coulda been something!"

Then something remarkable happened.

I was standing in Target's toy department when it hit me. Dominos would make a perfect border for a mosaic tile tabletop! I bought two sets of those magical little tiles. *This is going to be really fun,* I thought, *but first I need to teach myself how to mosaic tile.* I knew I'd better hurry. The countdown was on. I had about two weeks before I would be on to the next thing. Tie-dying perhaps?

Making a stop at the local home improvement store, I quickly stocked up on ceramic tiles, mastic, and grout. I scoured my junk room to find the random bits and pieces I needed to complete my creation. It was a good thing that I had saved some Monopoly game pieces, and a travel plate from Las Vegas. The hoarder inside me was finally getting the validation it desperately needed. That Las Vegas plate ended up being the perfect focal point of the piece. I dragged

the table up from the basement and set up shop in the kitchen. I found a hammer and a dishcloth to cover the plate and smashed it without a second thought. Experience has since taught me that

smashing away can be a very, very bad idea. But either luck or destiny was on my side that day. With dominos, china shards, and mastic in hand, I started filling the table-top with the random pieces. That's all it took—I was completely hooked!

Four hours later, all of the bits and pieces were in place. It took every ounce of patience I had to wait for the glue to dry so I could move on to the next step: grouting.

Twenty-four hours later, I grabbed a cup of coffee and the tile grout. I was so excited that a genuine danger existed of confusing the two. I sipped carefully. After reading the directions (I am female, after all), I told myself: *This doesn't seem so hard, just get out your rubber gloves and whip up a batch.* And that's exactly what I did. I grabbed an empty bucket and a pitcher of water and started to mix. When the grout looked close to the consistency

described on the box, I scooped up a handful and plopped it onto my creation. *What have I done?! My beautiful table is covered in mud!* I took a deep breath and tried to conjure up all the patience and faith that I possessed. *What's the worst thing that could happen?* I feebly reassured myself. *It's only a vintage table that I've carried around for close to a decade. I can always get another one.* Right?

What a mess.

As I grabbed my sponge and bucket, I could barely wait to see what lay hidden beneath the muddy mess. I had to remind myself to just keep wiping.

Lo and behold, it worked.

What a myriad of reactions I experienced! The feeling is difficult to describe, but this cocktail of elation, satisfaction, pride, relief, and early anticipation of my next project washes over me every time I remove grout from one of my mosaic tile pieces.

As most mosaic tile artists will tell you, grouting isn't their favorite part, but the final result is always worth the effort (unless you've chosen the wrong grout color . . . but that's another chapter).

So that's my story and I'm sticking to it. Who knows?

Perhaps by reading this book, you're ready to begin your own artist's journey.

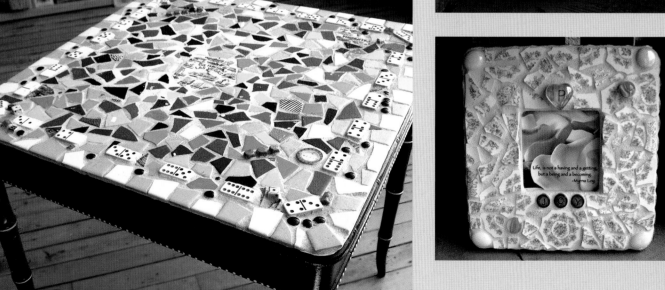